INTRODUCING ISSUES WITH OPPOSING VIEWPOINTS®

Classified Intelligence and Leaks

Lisa Idzikowski, Book Editor

GREENHAVEN PUBLISHING

Published in 2019 by Greenhaven Publishing, LLC
353 3rd Avenue, Suite 255, New York, NY 10010

First Edition

Library of Congress Cataloging-in-Publication Data

Names: Idzikowski, Lisa, editor.
Title: Classified intelligence and leaks / edited by Lisa Idzikowski.
Description: New York : Greenhaven Publishing, 2019. | Series: Introducing issues with opposing viewpoints | Includes bibliographic references and index. | Audience: Grades 7-12.
Identifiers: LCCN ISBN 9781534503571 (library bound) | ISBN 9781534503588 (pbk.)
Subjects: LCSH: Leaks (Disclosure of information)--United States. | Security classification (Government documents). | Government information--United States.
Classification: LCC JF1525.S4 C537 2019 | DDC 352.3/79--dc23

LC record available at https://lccn.loc.gov/2017061865

Manufactured in the United States of America

Website: http://greenhavenpublishing.com

Contents

Chapter 3: Can Anything Be Done to Prevent Leaks of Classified Intelligence?

Foreword

Indulging in a wide spectrum of ideas, beliefs, and perspectives is a critical cornerstone of democracy. After all, it is often debates over differences of opinion, such as whether to legalize abortion, how to treat prisoners, or when to enact the death penalty, that shape our society and drive it forward. Such diversity of thought is frequently regarded as the hallmark of a healthy and civilized culture. As the Reverend Clifford Schutjer of the First Congregational Church in Mansfield, Ohio, declared in a 2001 sermon, "Surrounding oneself with only like-minded people, restricting what we listen to or read only to what we find agreeable is irresponsible. Refusing to entertain doubts once we make up our minds is a subtle but deadly form of arrogance." With this advice in mind, Introducing Issues with Opposing Viewpoints books aim to open readers' minds to the critically divergent views that comprise our world's most important debates.

Introducing Issues with Opposing Viewpoints simplifies for students the enormous and often overwhelming mass of material now available via print and electronic media. Collected in every volume is an array of opinions that captures the essence of a particular controversy or topic. Introducing Issues with Opposing Viewpoints books embody the spirit of nineteenth-century journalist Charles A. Dana's axiom: "Fight for your opinions, but do not believe that they contain the whole truth, or the only truth." Absorbing such contrasting opinions teaches students to analyze the strength of an argument and compare it to its opposition. From this process readers can inform and strengthen their own opinions, or be exposed to new information that will change their minds. Introducing Issues with Opposing Viewpoints is a mosaic of different voices. The authors are statesmen, pundits, academics, journalists, corporations, and ordinary people who have felt compelled to share their experiences and ideas in a public forum. Their words have been collected from newspapers, journals, books, speeches, interviews, and the Internet, the fastest growing body of opinionated material in the world.

Introducing Issues with Opposing Viewpoints shares many of the well-known features of its critically acclaimed parent series, Opposing

Viewpoints. The articles allow readers to absorb and compare divergent perspectives. Active reading questions preface each viewpoint, requiring the student to approach the material thoughtfully and carefully. Photographs, charts, and graphs supplement each article. A thorough introduction provides readers with crucial background on an issue. An annotated bibliography points the reader toward articles, books, and websites that contain additional information on the topic. An appendix of organizations to contact contains a wide variety of charities, nonprofit organizations, political groups, and private enterprises that each hold a position on the issue at hand. Finally, a comprehensive index allows readers to locate content quickly and efficiently.

Introducing Issues with Opposing Viewpoints is also significantly different from Opposing Viewpoints. As the series title implies, its presentation will help introduce students to the concept of opposing viewpoints and learn to use this material to aid in critical writing and debate. The series' four-color, accessible format makes the books attractive and inviting to readers of all levels. In addition, each viewpoint has been carefully edited to maximize a reader's understanding of the content. Short but thorough viewpoints capture the essence of an argument. A substantial, thought-provoking essay question placed at the end of each viewpoint asks the student to further investigate the issues raised in the viewpoint, compare and contrast two authors' arguments, or consider how one might go about forming an opinion on the topic at hand. Each viewpoint contains sidebars that include at-a-glance information and handy statistics. A Facts About section located in the back of the book further supplies students with relevant facts and figures.

Following in the tradition of the Opposing Viewpoints series, Greenhaven Publishing continues to provide readers with invaluable exposure to the controversial issues that shape our world. As John Stuart Mill once wrote: "The only way in which a human being can make some approach to knowing the whole of a subject is by hearing what can be said about it by persons of every variety of opinion and studying all modes in which it can be looked at by every character of mind. No wise man ever acquired his wisdom in any mode but this." It is to this principle that Introducing Issues with Opposing Viewpoints books are dedicated.

Introduction

"Our democratic principles require that the American people be informed of the activities of their Government. Also, our Nation's progress depends on the free flow of information both within the Government and to the American people. Nevertheless, throughout our history, the national defense has required that certain information be maintained in confidence in order to protect our citizens, our democratic institutions, our homeland security, and our interactions with foreign nations. Protecting information critical to our Nation's security and demonstrating our commitment to open Government through accurate and accountable application of classification standards and routine, secure, and effective declassification are equally important priorities."

—President Barack Obama, Executive Order 13526, December 29, 2009

According to *Merriam-Webster,* if information is classified, it can be "withheld from general circulation for reasons of national security." Very likely, governments around the world would agree. They would assert that to protect their citizens, certain information or intelligence must be kept away from those sources who might seek to do harm. The United States is no different in this respect. As stated in his executive order, which currently governs issues of classified information, President Barack Obama maintained that "throughout our history, the national defense has required that certain information be maintained in confidence in order to protect our citizens, our democratic institutions, our homeland security, and our interactions with foreign nations."

To uphold this mandate, the United States has developed a network of security laws, guidelines, procedures, and practices. Three laws protect classified information: the Espionage Act, the Atomic Energy Act, and the Intelligence Identities Act. Throughout the nation a startling number of employees, supervisors, department managers, military, politicians, and countless other individuals toil daily to make the security machine function.

According to established practices, and outlined in Executive Order 13526, classified information could be concerned with various topics such as the military; intelligence sources, methods, and activities; nuclear capabilities or materials; or scientific and technological matters. Information determined to be worthy of classification is assigned to one of three categories. The designation of "Top Secret" is applied to information that if disclosed or made public without authorization could reasonably "be expected to cause exceptionally grave damage to the national security" The term "Secret" is applied to information that if disclosed or made public without authorization could "be expected to cause serious damage to the national security" And the label of "Confidential" is used to define information that "...could be expected to cause damage to the national security" if it fell into the wrong hands. Information that is designated "Top Secret" is the most sensitive or potentially damaging, followed by "Secret," leaving, "Confidential" the least sensitive category.

Of course, not all information generated by the government is vital to the nation's security. Other less crucial information may only be of importance to specific groups, such as law enforcement. This information could be labeled with assorted wording such as sensitive and not classified, or for official use only. At various times through the years, classified information has leaked out or been given to unauthorized individuals or groups. Sensationalist reports have sometimes accompanied these actions. The people leaking out the information have in some instances been hailed as heroes, scoffed at as ignorant, and even criticized as criminals.

The concerns of keeping classified information protected are real. Individuals that need to use it are screened by assorted means. Once individuals pass the screening measures they acquire a security clearance. It is estimated that nearly one million people in the United States have obtained top security clearance. Some people think that this makes the issue of protection very difficult. In a 2010 memo, Jacob J. Lew, Management and Budget Director from the Executive Office of the President, wrote that, "Our national defense requires that sensitive information be maintained in confidence to protect our citizens, our democratic institutions, and our homeland. Protecting information critical to our nation's security is the responsibility of each individual who is granted access to classified information. Any unauthorized disclosure of classified information is a violation of our law and compromises our national security."

Another concern voiced by some is that the United States has simply too much information labeled as classified. They argue that it waters down the entire system of classification. They even worry that the volume of unimportant information endangers that which is truly vital to national security. In an effort to help with this dilemma, Executive Order 13526 can again be consulted. It outlines ways to declassify or remove the classification label of information. The order also outlines procedures for newly classified material in that it must be marked for declassification within a specific time frame, and that no information shall remain classified forever.

A case in point from 2011 neatly demonstrates declassification. Six previously secret documents from 1917, the time period of World War I (1914–1918), were released from classification. The information details the composition and techniques of secret writing and invisible ink. The US Central Intelligence Agency (CIA) determined that the documents no longer were sensitive or necessary to keep secret. CIA director Leon Panetta stated that the "documents remained classified for nearly a century until recent advancements in technology made it possible to release them."

Many knowledgeable individuals agree that the issues surrounding classified intelligence and information are complex. They involve not only the United States acting alone in its best interest. They also comprise an important issue that affects both cooperating nations around the world and those opposed to each other. The current debate that surrounds the issue of classified intelligence is explored in the viewpoints that make up *Introducing Issues with Opposing Viewpoints: Classified Intelligence and Leaks*, shedding light on this complicated and ongoing contemporary issue.

Chapter 1

Is All Intelligence Classified?

How much information should be shared with the American public?

Viewpoint 1

Not All Government Documents Should Be Classified

"Overclassification is rampant, and nearly everyone who works with classified information recognizes the problem."

Elizabeth Goitein and David M. Shapiro

In the following viewpoint, Elizabeth Goitein and David M. Shapiro contend that even though information is protected through the classification system for the safety of the United States, too much is classified. According to the authors overclassification is actually dangerous. Goitein and Shapiro support these claims with various examples and they analyze the reasons causing this dangerous predicament. Goitein is codirector of the Brennan Center for Justice and Shapiro is a lawyer who once worked for Brennan Center's Liberty and National Security Program.

AS YOU READ, CONSIDER THE FOLLOWING QUESTIONS:

1. What types of problems does overclassification cause?
2. What is not being followed that might alter this problem?
3. Give two examples cited in the article of incentives that encourage overclassification.

"Reducing Overclassification Through Accountability," by Elizabeth (Liza) Goitein, and David M. Shapiro, The Brennan Center for Justice at New York University School of Law, October 5, 2011. Reprinted with permission.

The authority to classify documents exists to protect information that could threaten national security if it got into the wrong hands. It is one of the most important tools our government has to keep us safe. But many secrets "protected" by the classification system pose no danger to the nation's safety.

On the contrary, needless classification—"overclassification"—jeopardizes national security. Excessive secrecy prevents federal agencies from sharing information internally, with other agencies, and with state and local law enforcement, making it more difficult to draw connections and anticipate threats. The 9/11 Commission found that the failure to share information contributed to intelligence gaps in the months before the September 11, 2001, attacks, cautioning that "[c]urrent security requirements nurture overclassification and excessive compartmentation of information among agencies."

Overclassification also corrodes democratic government. Secret programs stifled public debate on the decisions that shaped our response to the September 11 attacks. Should the military and CIA have used torture to extract information from detainees in secret overseas prisons and at Guantánamo Bay? Should the National Security Agency have eavesdropped on Americans' telephone calls without warrants? Even leaving aside the legality of these measures, whether to use torture or to forego the use of warrants are questions that, in a democracy, properly belong in the public sphere. Classification forced the nation to rely on leaked information to debate these questions, and to do so well after torture and warrantless surveillance programs were in place.

Improving the System

Overclassification is rampant, and nearly everyone who works with classified information recognizes the problem. In 1993, Senator John Kerry, who reviewed classified documents while chairing the Senate Select Committee on POW/MIA Affairs, commented, "I do not think more than a hundred, or a couple of hundred, pages of the thousands of [classified] documents we looked at had any current classification importance…." And two years later, Donald Rumsfeld, while noting that disclosure of truly sensitive information can put lives at risk, acknowledged, "I have long believed that

Some experts believe that overclassification of intelligence jeopardized national security regarding the 9/11 attacks.

too much material is classified across the federal government as a general rule."

Government statistics bear out these assessments. When a member of the public asks an agency to review particular records for declassification (through a process called "mandatory declassification review"),

92 percent of the time the agency determines that at least some of the requested records need not remain classified. But the number of documents reviewed through this process pales in comparison to the universe of documents that, though they may not require classification, remain unreviewed—and thus classified—for many years.

A major theme of this report—and a source of frustration to those who have studied the classification system—is the persistent gap between written regulation and actual practice. Chief executives since Franklin Delano Roosevelt have issued executive orders on classification. Classification authority emanates primarily from these orders, which have long purported to impose common-sense limits, such as a ban on using classification to conceal embarrassing information about government officials. And the current order—Executive Order 13,526, which President Obama issued in December 2009—includes further limits, such as a requirement that records not be classified if significant doubt exists about the need for secrecy. In practice, however, such limits too often fall by the wayside. As a Senate Commission chaired by Daniel Patrick Moynihan found, "Any policy, including on classification and declassification, is only as good as its implementation."

This report focuses on improved implementation, i.e., how to make sure that classifiers comply with existing criteria for classifying documents. It does not address ways in which the classification system could be improved by changing those criteria, such as revising agency classification guides—which govern many classification decisions—to eliminate classification categories that are outdated, unnecessary, or imprecise; requiring classifiers to weigh national security risks against the public interest in disclosure; or amending the National Security Act of 1947 to clarify that "intelligence sources and methods" may be classified only if their disclosure would harm national security. Measures to improve the substantive criteria for classification will form a critical piece of any successful reform effort, and their omission from this report should not be taken as an assessment of their relative importance. But the widespread failure of classifiers to comply with existing rules suggests that changing them will have little effect until we understand and address the persistent gap between rules and reality.

This report concludes that the primary source of the "implementation gap" is the skewed incentive structure underlying the current system—a structure that all but guarantees overclassification will occur. Numerous incentives push powerfully in the direction of classification, including the culture of secrecy that pervades some government agencies; the desire to conceal information that would reveal governmental misconduct or incompetence; the relative ease with which executive officials can implement policy when involvement by other officials, members of Congress, and the public is limited; the pressure to err on the side of classification rather than risk official sanctions or public condemnation for revealing sensitive information; and the simple press of business, which discourages giving thoughtful consideration to classification decisions. By contrast, there are essentially no incentives to refrain from or challenge improper classification. After all, classification is an easy exercise that can be accomplished with little effort or reflection; those who classify documents improperly are rarely if ever held accountable—indeed, there is no reliable mechanism in place to identify them; classifiers receive insufficient training in the limits of their authority; and those who have access to classified information are neither encouraged to challenge improper classification decisions nor rewarded for doing so.

FAST FACT

In 1951, President Truman was the first president to sign an executive order governing classification of information.

Skewed Incentives

In order to succeed, any effort to reduce overclassification must address this problem of skewed incentives. The final chapter of this report sets forth a reform proposal that would rebalance existing incentives, primarily by introducing accountability into the classification system. The proposal consists of six main parts:

1. When classifying documents, officials would be required to complete short electronic forms in which they would provide explanations for their classification decisions.

2. In each agency with classification authority, the Office of the Inspector General would conduct "spot audits" of classifiers, identifying those who exhibit serious tendencies to overclassify and subjecting them to periodic follow-up audits.

3. Successive unsatisfactory audit results would result in mandatory escalating consequences for the individual classifier, agency management, and the agency itself.

4. Agencies would be required to spend at least eight percent of their security classification budgets on training and to obtain approval of their training materials from the government office that oversees classification.

5. Derivative classifiers (those who carry forward classification decisions made by others) would be "held harmless" if they failed to classify information whose status was ambiguous.

6. Agencies would establish procedures to allow authorized holders of classified information to challenge classification decisions anonymously, and those who brought successful challenges would be given small cash awards.

We recommend that this proposal be implemented as a pilot project at one or more agencies. This could be accomplished largely if not exclusively through executive order and implementing regulation. The results of the project should be closely tracked and evaluated to assess both its benefits and its costs. If the proposal yields the expected dividends, it could be expanded through legislation. One thing is certain: the status quo is untenable. The classification system must be reformed if we are to preserve the critical role that transparent government plays in a functioning democracy.

EVALUATING THE AUTHORS' ARGUMENTS:

In this viewpoint, Goitein and Shapiro suggest that a "skewed incentive structure" may be the cause of over classification of information. If this is so, how might their suggested improvements work for the system?

Viewpoint 2

Can the Overclassification Dilemma Be Fixed?

"[The] call for agencies to take a leading role in reducing the amount of information that is classified is potentially a game changer."

Aaron Mackey

In the following viewpoint, Aaron Mackey comments on then-Director of National Intelligence James Clapper's call to overhaul the government system used to classify intelligence information. Mackey is clearly pleased to report the possible changes and problem solutions that Clapper envisioned during the Obama administration. However, he acknowledges that implementation of the solutions is the key to success and might prove to be a challenge. Aaron Mackey writes for the Electronic Frontier Foundation (EFF).

AS YOU READ, CONSIDER THE FOLLOWING QUESTIONS:

1. What is one function of the Director of National Intelligence, according to Mackey's report?
2. According to Mackey, what did James Clapper do to overhaul governmental secrecy?
3. Explain one solution to the overclassification problem as reported by Mackey.

"Is the U.S Intelligence Chief Serious About Fixing Overclassification? Time Will Tell, by Aaron Mackey, Electronic Frontier Foundation, April 11, 2016. https://www.eff.org/deeplinks/2016/04/us-intelligence-chief-serious-about-fixing-overclassification-time-will-tell.

Critics charge that the US government is remarkably secretive for a country that purports to be open and free. Reducing overclassification could change that.

EFF has long been critical of overbroad government secrecy, which has been used to cover up everything from illegal activities to questionable legal justifications for mass surveillance.

Given that government officials default to withholding important details from the public regarding national security, we were pleasantly surprised to read a memo that Director of National Intelligence James Clapper sent to intelligence agencies last month.

Clapper's memo directs the heads of several intelligence agencies, including the NSA and CIA, to substantially overhaul the government's formal classification system as part of a process known as the Fundamental Classification Guidance Review.

Although the review sounds like a routine bureaucratic exercise, Clapper's call for agencies to take a leading role in reducing the amount of information that is classified is potentially a game changer.

Fast Fact

According to the Oxford English Dictionary, starting in 1940, the term "classified," referred to something officially secret.

It is refreshing to see the country's intelligence chief acknowledge that the government makes too much information secret via its arcane classification rules. Even better: Clapper went beyond merely admitting that too much information is classified and actually suggested some concrete solutions, including:

- Requiring discretionary declassification. Intelligence agencies would proactively identify and declassify documents, which would be a marked change. Although agencies already have the discretion to declassify information on their own, Clapper's memo calls for a new approach that would focus agencies on disclosing more records.
- Eliminating the "confidential" category of classified information. Clapper asks the agencies to consider whether the lowest level of classification can be eliminated to "promote transparency." The confidential label was placed on 22% of the total material that agencies initially classified in fiscal year 2014.
- Reducing the number of people who can classify material. Clapper states that agencies should reduce the number of officials within each agency who have the authority to classify information "to the minimum number required."
- Creating more uniform classification rules. The memo asks for agencies to comment on creating a classification guide that would be used for classification issues common to the agencies. As it stands now, agencies develop their own classifications guidelines.

The true impact of Clapper's proposals will depend on how they are implemented. If done correctly they have the potential to reduce the amount of material kept secret by intelligence agencies.

For example, if proactive discretionary disclosure requires agencies to presume that there is a public interest in disclosing the records that must be outweighed by a concrete risk of harming national security, it could lead to greater disclosure. Similarly, if material previously marked "confidential" now must be made public, that would undoubtedly be progress.

At the same time, discretionary disclosure without a strong presumption that material must be made public is a hollow effort to increase transparency. And without clear guidance to agencies about eliminating the "confidential" category of classification, they may simply mark the same materials with the next-highest classification category rather than disclose the information.

Nonetheless, EFF appreciates Clapper's candor and leadership in admitting that the government classifies too much information. Indeed, President Obama recently explained that his own experiences have led him to the same conclusion about the government's overclassification.

EFF is hopeful that Clapper and President Obama's comments indicate that they are both serious about reforming the current classification system. We look forward to seeing whether agencies take Clapper's requests seriously and if it ultimately results in less government secrecy.

EVALUATING THE AUTHOR'S ARGUMENTS:

In this viewpoint, Aaron Mackey implies that he is interested in the solutions posed by James Clapper. Compare the solutions provided in this viewpoint with those of the previous viewpoint by Goitein and Shapiro.

Viewpoint 3

Obtaining Information Through Surveillance Is Beneficial but Comes with Challenges

"Surveillance is, quite simply, observations conducted to gain information."

Brian D. Baker and Whitney D. Gunter

In the following viewpoint, Brian D. Baker and Whitney D. Gunter maintain that surveillance is simply the act of obtaining information. But what if surveillance intrudes the reasonable privacy of a group or individual? Baker and Gunter analyze the goals, types, beneficial reasons and concerns surrounding surveillance. Brian D. Baker is a Certified Protection Professional and a Certified Protection Officer. Whitney D. Gunter is a Certified Protection Officer and a graduate in criminal justice.

"Surveillance: Concepts and Practices for Fraud, Security and Crime Investigation," by Brian D. Baker and Whitney D. Gunter, International Foundation for Protection Officers, August 2005. Reprinted by permission.

AS YOU READ, CONSIDER THE FOLLOWING QUESTIONS:

1. What are the benefits of surveillance as reported by Baker and Gunter?
2. Identify the three intelligence gathering agencies as stated by Baker and Gunter.
3. How can surveillance affect the investigator according to Baker and Gunter?

Surveillance is, quite simply, observations conducted to gain information. This simple definition includes a plethora of techniques and methods that can be considered a form of surveillance.

Many of these are recognizable through common knowledge produced by popular culture. The most well known methods include stationary surveillance, technical surveillance (typically covert video or audio recordings), electronic surveillance (digital observations, keystroke counting), and many more. Nearly anyone can engage in surveillance once properly trained and educated; individuals using the various techniques of surveillance range from federal officials trying to save lives from terrorists and other criminals to private investigators gathering evidence for civil court.

One of the most versatile and important skills any investigator can possess is surveillance. Communications skills involving interviewing and report writing are usually thought of as the most critical investigative competencies. The primary skill used in surveillance is the power of observation, which always precedes reporting. Surveillance, being such an important part of investigation, is a topic that should not be taken lightly. It is important for investigators to understand when surveillance should be used, the objectives of surveillance, stress related to surveillance, and ethical/legal concerns about surveillance.

Depending of the type of investigation, there are many reasons why surveillance can be beneficial. The objectives of surveillance will vary from case to case, but are most often one or more of following:

- Obtain information for a search or warrant.
- Locate a subject, contraband, or the site of illegal activities.

When it comes to surveillance, it's a fine line between maintaining security and violating citizens' privacy.

- Obtain intelligence about a subject, criminal group or location.
- Prevent a crime from occurring through covert or overt surveillance. Gather intelligence for a raid.
- Provide protection for informants, undercover individuals or others.

Additionally, many cases end with no observations made. The credible report of no observations may be useful in re-evaluating the method of investigation, the feasibility of surveillance at a particular day or time of day. A lack of observations can also reinforce the positive information indicating that a situation is innocent, legitimate, non-criminal, or beneficial to the client or corporate interest.

The Goal of Surveillance

The observation and reporting mission of private security applies to surveillance. Most surveillance operatives are private investigators, security officers (including retail security and patrol officers), and corporate investigators. While the surveillance role of a police investigator is one of many duties, the specialty of surveillance is more prevalent in private security. As noted in the Protection Officer Training

Manual (2003), security officers outnumber law enforcement officers three to one. Operational budgets mirror this statistic, which is relevant to the importance of security officers and particularly the proactive side of asset protection.

The role of the surveillance investigator is to collect information for the furtherance of an investigation. Most cases do not transition from a stationary surveillance to a felony traffic stop, as popular belief would suggest. Accurate observation and credible reporting should be considered the final product and the overall objective of a successful surveillance case. The differences between police and security help to clarify the importance of surveillance in the investigative process. Surveillance may be considered a skill or a task for the police officer. The police officer is, in most cases, reactive to a situation with the intention of apprehension and prosecution of the offender. Private security is more function specific, being the protection of an organization through proactive and preventive services. The function of a private investigator is more specific and more reliant on the specific tasks of observation and surveillance.

There are other forms of government law enforcement beyond policing that private investigators should also understand. This part of law enforcement involves surveillance and other intelligence gathering in a primarily proactive (prevention of crimes) method. The Federal Bureau of Investigations (FBI) is the most recognized intelligence-gathering agency, but there are many others, such as Alcohol Tobacco and Firearms (ATF), the Secret Service, and investigations divisions of federal agencies, state agencies and police departments. The functions of these agencies/divisions are often a blend of reactive (law enforcement) and proactive (security) goals.

As previously addressed, many cases end positively with a lack of observations. The belief that every surveillance case will detect fraud or result in an arrest is a mistake often fueled by Hollywood fiction. Practitioners in the criminal justice system commonly agree that the image of investigators presented by the entertainment industry fills students with false hopes and provides clients or outsiders with unrealistic goals. Surveillance should be judged as a success whenever the outcome of the assignment assists the investigation with credible information or circumstances that contribute to a more credible assessment of the purpose of the investigation. If the surveillance operative is further able to have personal growth from the learning experience or practice of the art of surveillance, then the activity should be considered a personal success, not a waste of time or resources.

Surveillance as Qualitative Analysis

There are many uses for surveillance, including both criminal and civil matters. However, there is also another purpose that is not often discussed. Surveillance can also be used as a method of systemic observation for professional research. This can be accomplished in many fields, not just criminal justice. Businesses often conduct "focus groups" to determine consumer opinions; many of these are accompanied with covert or overt observations recorded to determine consumer reactions. This can lead to more accurate observations when combined with verbalized opinions. Quantitative analysis (using math to prove something is occurring more often than by coincidence) is currently most popular among social science researchers. This provides proof that observations are more than just anecdotal evidence. However, many observations are too specific or too rare to be measured with numbers. These types of observations are called qualitative observations and are sometimes required for research. Surveillance is often a part of these observations, especially covert surveillance that would not change a subject's behavior. Because quantitative analysis is the "golden standard" today, many investigators are, unfortunately, being discouraged from using qualitative methods for research. However, using surveillance for qualitative analysis and, occasionally, as a source for data used in quantitative methods is often required and useful. Therefore, understanding the concepts of surveillance is helpful not only to full-time investigators, but also to professionals seeking to research any number of topics in nearly any field.

Physical Stress and Mental Stress

Surveillance is defined as covert observations of places and persons for the purpose of obtaining information (Dempsey, 2003). The term covert infers that the operative conducting the surveillance is

Fast Fact

According to a 2015 Pew Research Center poll, 54% of Americans disapprove of governmental collection of phone and internet data.

discreet and secretive. Surveillance that maintains a concealed, hidden, undetected nature clearly has the greatest chance of success because the subject of the surveillance will act or perform naturally. Remaining undetected during covert surveillance work often involves physical fatigue, mental stress, and very challenging situations.

[...]

Variables in Surveillance

So much has been written about surveillance that another chapter about paying attention to detail and staying alert may be considered repetitious. Surveillance is challenging in the competitive arena of one human versus another, animal against animal. It is a game of watching others without being noticed and a game of gathering facts without appearing to care. The investigator must appear non-threatening or risk being compromised. Some situations permit an investigator to sit in the front seat of a car and videotape a subject 20 feet away without any fear of detection. Other times, however, an investigator may have a claims conscious subject smile and wave hello through the viewfinder of the same camera over a block away. Surveillance is like a masterpiece painting that changes with only the slightest stroke of the brush or the angle of the lighting. Everyone has a similar perspective to approaching the challenge, but it is the artist's skill that affects perspective and will elevate a painter to the level of artist, much in the same way that it is the operative's skill that will elevate him/her to the level of investigator.

[...]

Obtaining Information

How can one observe accurately? Does the investigator know what he or she is seeing? This is a question that may be answered by understanding the purpose of the investigation and by having good intelligence prior to starting the investigation. Good intelligence prior to starting an investigation appears to be a contradiction to the fact that the purpose of surveillance is to gathering intelligence. However, every investigator must at least know a few things about the case before starting surveillance. Failure to have basic intelligence on the subject, location, and purpose of the investigation could result in failure and result in the investigator being discovered, hurt or killed.

[...]

Ethical Concerns

Surveillance should never intrude on the subject's reasonable expectation of privacy. If the investigator is utilizing technology to observe into the subject's life where one normally could not observe, then perhaps there is an issue of privacy intrusion. Utilizing a digital zoom to see through sheer curtains of a living room and observe into a house, observing what is happening in the hallway or a back bedroom, may be considered a use of unique means that may be an invasion of privacy. An investigator that rents a bucket truck to ascend a utility pole, just to look over the subject's 7-foot privacy fence is going to extraordinary means and may be violating privacy. Although private security and surveillance operatives are not police officers with the primary concern over search and seizure protections, if there is a violation of a subject's rights through unreasonable means, there will likely be civil liability.

[...]

An investigator must establish the surveillance location from the same vantage point that any non-investigator with a legitimate reason for being there could have the same observation. The investigator must answer the question, "If someone walked down the street, would they be able to observe the same thing that I see?" When doing surveillance around a corporate facility, there are far greater options for hiding or concealment but the concept of expectation of privacy still applies. Hiding in a locker in a changing room would be a violation if there is an expectation that workers may use the area to change clothes. The expectation of privacy in the workplace is generally at a lower standard than around a person's residence, but an expectation exists regardless.

[...]

Investigators should conduct surveillance discreetly and surveillance should represent the subject in as natural a manner and environment as possible. Cutting a subject's tire for the purpose of filming him changing that tire is an example of unethical and criminal conduct. Dumping a handful of change onto the ground around the subject's vehicle, just to film her stooping to pick up the change is unethical and presents a situation that is unnatural. An investigator must be able to say under oath that the observed actions were not in any way influenced by the investigator's presence.

Conclusions and Final Thoughts

Surveillance is not an easy task and is not always exciting. The goals and objectives often vary from case to case, as do the applicable methods of surveillance. Understanding how to be best prepared for surveillance and what the objectives are can help make the job easier and more beneficial. To be a successful investigator, experience is a requirement. There is no substitute for experience, but research can be a good starting point.

EVALUATING THE AUTHOR'S ARGUMENTS:

In this viewpoint, Brian D. Baker and Whitney D. Gunter explain the basic techniques and goals of surveillance. Compare and contrast the benefits of surveillance with its challenges.

Viewpoint 4

Surveillance and Gathering of Private Information Is Necessary to Aid Counterterrorism Efforts

"In the wake of the September 11 attacks, Congress passed sweeping legislation to bolster U.S. counterterrorism efforts."

Council on Foreign Relations

In the following viewpoint, editors from the Council on Foreign Relations analyze the issue of surveillance and its use in counterterrorism efforts. Defenders of surveillance say it helps uncover terrorist plots, while opponents argue that it infringes on the civil liberties of citizens. The authors examine the controversies and challenges under the recent administrations of Presidents Bush and Obama and look to the future. The Council on Foreign Relations is a nonpartisan think tank that specializes in US foreign policy.

AS YOU READ, CONSIDER THE FOLLOWING QUESTIONS:

1. According to the Newsteam Staff, what method of surveillance is used under the USA PATRIOT Act?
2. What kind of surveillance is being used, and what results are obtained according to Newsteam?
3. What Fourth Amendment rights are suffering because of surveillance programs as stated by the authors?

In the wake of the September 11 attacks, Congress passed sweeping legislation to bolster U.S. counterterrorism efforts. Some of the most controversial measures, including the 2001 USA PATRIOT Act, significantly enhanced the federal government's ability to collect and analyze private information related to U.S. citizens. Proponents argue that the broader surveillance authorities are required to uncover and neutralize terrorism plots, while critics say the expanded powers infringe on civil liberties.

In 2005, the Bush administration came under fire from Democrats and activist groups after press reports disclosed the National Security Agency's warrantless wiretapping program. In 2013, the Obama administration similarly attracted criticism from watchdog groups upon leaks related to its far-reaching domestic surveillance activities under the NSA. The episode has revived debate over privacy and national security and raised calls for reform.

What Is the Domestic Surveillance Controversy Under Obama?

Two NSA surveillance programs were exposed in press reports in June 2013. First, a *Guardian* report disclosed a classified Foreign Intelligence Surveillance Court (FISC) order instructing Verizon, one of the largest U.S. telecommunications firms, to hand over phone records of millions of Americans to the NSA. Another secret program, code-named PRISM, accessed troves of communication data—audio/video chats, emails, photos, and other media—from several U.S. technology companies, according to the *Washington Post*. Subsequent leaks revealed details on additional programs that gave

President George W. Bush signed the USA PATRIOT Act into law in October 2001 in response to the terrorist attacks that shook the United States on September 11 of that year.

the NSA extensive electronic surveillance tools, both domestic and international, allowing the government to track and tap into conversations of suspected terrorists, civilians, and even friendly foreign heads of state.

Amid criticism from civil rights groups, the Obama administration initially defended the surveillance program, saying it is legal, limited, and effective in preventing terrorist attacks. Director of National Intelligence James Clapper said the program does not monitor phone calls, but acquires telephony metadata to be queried only when there is a "reasonable suspicion" of links to a foreign terrorist organization.

Experts say the White House is likely relying on Section 215 of the Patriot Act, a provision that says government can mandate the turnover of "any tangible things" from any entity as long as the items are for an investigation to defend against international terrorism or spying. In congressional testimony, NSA chief Gen. Keith Alexander credited his agency's surveillance with helping prevent "dozens" of terrorist attacks, and said he welcomed a debate on the legality of the programs.

In August, President Obama created a task force of intelligence and legal experts to review NSA operations and recommend potential reforms. The inquiry is reportedly part of a comprehensive White House review of signals intelligence.

What Was the Domestic Surveillance Controversy Under Bush?

After 9/11, the Bush administration opted not to seek approval from the FISC before intercepting "international communications into and out of the United States of persons linked to al-Qaeda (PDF) or related terrorist organizations." The special secret court, set up in 1978 following previous administrations' domestic spying abuses, was designed to act as a neutral overseer in granting government agencies surveillance authorization.

After the NSA program was revealed by the *New York Times* in late 2005, former attorney general Alberto R. Gonzales argued (PDF) that President Bush had the legal authority under the constitution and congressional statute to conduct warrantless surveillance on U.S. persons "reasonably believed to be linked to al-Qaeda." The 2001 Authorization for Use of Military Force (AUMF), without specifically mentioning wiretapping, grants the president broad authority to use all necessary force "against those nations, organizations, or persons he determines planned, authorized, committed, or aided the [9/11] terrorist attacks." This includes, administration officials say, the powers to secretly gather domestic intelligence on al-Qaeda and associated groups.

Fast Fact

The USA PATRIOT Act of 2001 is a law that attempts to protect Americans by detecting and preventing terrorism.

The Bush administration maintained that the Foreign Intelligence Surveillance Act (FISA) was an outdated law-enforcement mechanism that was too time-consuming given the highly fluid, modern threat environment. Administration officials portrayed the NSA program as an "early warning system" (PDF) with "a military nature that requires speed and agility." Moreover, the White House stressed that the program was one not of domestic surveillance but of monitoring terrorists abroad, and publicly referred to the operation as the "Terrorist Surveillance Program." Opponents of the program referred to it as "domestic spying."

Under congressional pressure, Gonzales announced in January 2007 plans to disband the warrantless surveillance program and cede oversight to FISC, but questions about the legality of the program lingered in Congress and Gonzales resigned months later.

But Washington's vow to seek FISA approval for domestic surveillance was short-lived. In July 2007—weeks before Gonzales stepped down—intelligence officials pressed lawmakers for emergency legislation to broaden their wiretapping authority following a ruling by the court overseeing FISA that impacted the government's ability to intercept foreign communications passing through telecommunications "switches" on U.S. soil.

In August, President Bush signed the Protect America Act of 2007, which gave the attorney general and the director of national intelligence temporary power to approve international surveillance, rather than the special intelligence court. It also said warrants are unnecessary for surveillance of a person "reasonably believed" to be located overseas. This six-month stopgap measure expired in early 2008, but the FISA Amendments Act passed just months later contained similar provisions. President Obama reauthorized this legislation for five more years in December 2012.

Why Did this Become an Issue in Mid-2013?

Edward Snowden, the ex-CIA and former NSA contractor who leaked news of the two NSA programs, cited concerns over civil liberties violations as his primary motive. "The NSA has built an infrastructure that allows it to intercept almost everything. With this capability, the vast majority of human communications are automatically ingested without targeting. If I wanted to see your emails or your wife's phone, all I have to do is use intercepts. I can get your emails, passwords, phone records, credit cards," he said in an interview with the *Guardian*.

However, DNI Director Clapper publicly denied initial media reports (PDF) that the PRISM surveillance program was "an undisclosed collection or data mining program" that unilaterally taps into servers of U.S. telecoms. Rather, he stated the NSA program was limited and had been "widely known and publicly discussed since its inception in 2008." Specifically, Clapper said the program operated under Section 702 of FISA that permits the targeting of non-U.S. persons abroad without individualized court orders. As noted above, President Obama has reauthorized this legislation until 2017.

Many U.S. lawmakers have pressed for Snowden's prosecution, and the Obama administration referred his case to the Justice Department. Snowden fled to Hong Kong in May and was granted temporary asylum in Russia in August after spending weeks at the Moscow airport.

What Are the Challenges to Domestic Surveillance Policy?

Both Democratic and Republican lawmakers have called for a reexamination of the government's broad surveillance powers in the wake of disclosures regarding NSA activities. Top-ranking Senators Dianne Feinstein (D-CA) and John McCain (R-AZ) supported requests for congressional hearings on NSA surveillance, despite their support for the controversial programs. Sen. Ron Wyden (D-OR), an outspoken critic of NSA's broad authorities, has called on the White House to detail the extent to which Americans were monitored. In the past, the NSA said it lacked the technical ability to quantify this data.

Critics allege that even if the programs are operating within the letter of law, as the Obama administration says, they violate the law's intent and the values of democratic society. Some civil liberties activists have appealed for a thorough review of several provisions in the Patriot Act and FISA Amendments Act that provide controversial surveillance authorities.

Civil libertarians question whether government surveillance programs violate the Fourth Amendment to the U.S. Constitution, which states: "The right of the people to be secure in their persons, houses, papers, and effects, against unreasonable searches and seizures, shall not be violated, and no Warrants shall issue, but upon probable cause, supported by Oath or affirmation, and particularly describing the place to be searched, and the persons or things to be seized."

In December, Judge Richard J. Leon of the Federal District Court for the District of Columbia ruled that the NSA's bulk gathering of U.S. telephone metadata likely violates the Constitution. "Surely, such a program infringes on 'that degree of privacy' that the founders enshrined in the Fourth Amendment," he wrote. The judge ordered the government to stop collecting data on calls of the two plaintiffs in the case, but stayed the injunction to allow the government a chance to appeal. Other legal challenges are in early phases, including suits by the American Civil Liberties Union and the Electronic Frontier Foundation.

The Obama administration's task force also released its findings in December, recommending dozens of changes to current surveillance practice. Significant proposed reforms include: ending the government's indiscrimate collection of U.S. telephone metadata and requiring authorities to obtain a court order to query this information, held in the private sector; placing new limits on the monitoring of foreign leaders and ordinary non-Americans; and supporting new encryption standards and technologies. But legal analysts say that while the recommendations, if implemented, would require greater executive, congressional, and judicial review of surveillance activities, they would end few programs.

Meanwhile, in Congress, two bills that would forbid the NSA from collecting phone data on Americans not suspected of a crime are still in the early legislative process. The USA Freedom Act, which would reform the Patriot Act to address privacy concerns, has enough support to pass, but lawmakers are uncertain when it will be ready for a vote. Still, many Democrats and Republicans say the NSA programs are essential counterterrorism tools that have proved effective in preventing potential attacks.

EVALUATING THE AUTHOR'S ARGUMENTS:

In this viewpoint, the Council on Foreign Relations analyzes the challenges of surveillance and the actions taken by the government. Choose a side, either pro or con and using two or more facts from the article, defend your position.

Viewpoint 5

Citizens Have a Right to Know

Jamie Williams

"Secret law runs rampant in the United States, particularly when national security is concerned."

In the following viewpoint, Jamie Williams argues that in addition to secrecy surrounding national security and surveillance, a web of secret laws has entwined governmental practices in the United States. Williams maintains that these secret laws that blossomed after the September 11 terrorist attacks have given rise to massive spying programs that ensnare records of innocent people. Williams demands that changes occur but worries that such practices are becoming the new normal. Jamie Williams is an attorney who works for the Electronic Frontier Foundation as part of their civil liberties team.

AS YOU READ, CONSIDER THE FOLLOWING QUESTIONS:

1. As outlined by Williams, how has secret law permeated the government?
2. According to Williams, what should President Obama have done before leaving office?
3. What is PRISM, and how does it affect Americans as stated by Williams.

"The Problem of Our Surveillance Laws: Report Exposes Deeply Rooted Governmental Secrecy—Underscoring Why Obama Should Act Now," by Jamie Williams, Electronic Frontier Foundation, December 2, 2016. https://www.eff.org/deeplinks/2016/12/problem-our-surveillance-laws-report-exposes-deeply-rooted-governmental-secrecy.

The FBI has a long history of surveillance of notable individuals, but since 9/11 average Americans have been caught up in the government's surveillance efforts.

Kafka wrote in his parable The Problem of Our Laws, "It is an extremely painful thing to be ruled by laws that one does not know."

By this standard, America has long been in pain. Secret law runs rampant in the United States, particularly when national security is concerned. It may be legitimate for the government to keep some information secret, like targets of investigations and specific intelligence strategies, but this should be a relatively short list. And it should not, except in the most extreme circumstance, extend to the law itself. A recent report by the Brennan Center for Justice's Liza Goitein, however, exposes just how deep the problem of keeping even the law secret runs—with over-classification fostering constitutionally suspect legal reasoning and the rapid erosion of any meaningful check on governmental power.

The Brennan Center report also confirms something we've been arguing for years—it's time for some transparency and accountability in our laws. With only 48 days left in Obama's presidency, the call to shed some light on the law purportedly supporting the government's secret surveillance programs is all the more urgent. Opening the blinds is a practical step for protecting the democratic principles this country was founded on—especially as the power to invoke secrecy and surveil Americans is posed to pass into new and untested hands. President Obama, the time is now.

FAST FACT

In a 2017 poll by Pew Research, only 20 percent of Americans trust the government to do what's right.

The Report: The New Era of Secret Law

The Brennan Center report, entitled "The New Era of Secret Law," defines "secret law" as "any law withheld from the public." It outlines the dramatic post-9/11 expansion of the national security establishment's web of secret court decisions, regulations, and policies. The expansion of secret law implicates all three branches of government: the legislative branch, with secret legislative histories and classified committee reports incorporated by reference into bills and therefore vested with the force of law; the executive branch, with its classified presidential directives and secret binding legal interpretations by the Justice Department's Office of Legal Counsel (OLC); and the judicial branch, with the United States Foreign Intelligence Surveillance Court (FISC or FISA Court) issuing dozens of secret "ground-breaking" legal interpretations approving unprecedented mass surveillance programs—most of which opinions remain undisclosed to this day.

The report highlights that, while over-classification long been a problem, the national security establishment's intense, purposeful secrecy around the law post-9/11 is unprecedented in American history—representing a "significant departure from the commitment to openness and transparency that marked this country's first two centuries[.]" And it's a problem because secret law "interferes with the normal process by which law and legal interpretations are corrected or improved." It is impossible for citizens to challenge laws they are not aware of. Secrecy permits government actors "to develop unfair laws and to apply them [in] an unfair manner, safe in the knowledge that there will be no repercussions."

And it's true: as a result of pervasive, purposeful secrecy, the government's interpretation of our surveillance laws has grown increasingly distorted and unfair over time—now relied upon to justify mass spying programs that sweep up communications records of millions of innocent people.

What the American Public Deserves to Know—Now

President Obama has the opportunity to shed some light on secret surveillance law. EFF recently joined other civil liberties organizations in urging him to seize that opportunity—by taking a few concrete and important steps before he leaves office to release information about the relationship between the law and government spying. These are steps that will empower the American public and ensure that our government continues to function as the democracy our founding fathers intended.

Specifically, Obama should declassify and release to the public all of the following before January 20, 2017, redacting only information truly necessary to protect national security:

- All FISA Court opinions with a significant construction or interpretation of law, regardless of whether they were issued before the passage of the USA FREEDOM Act in 2015. As the Brennan Center report notes, there is "a backlog of significant FISA Court opinions that have yet to be declassified and released." These opinions are critical for understanding how the government's legal justification for mass spying has evolved over time—and where it has gone wrong.
- Office of Legal Counsel opinions related to national security and civil liberties. As noted above, OLC opinions contain binding legal interpretation, just as court decisions; that's why the OLC is sometimes referred to as having a "quasi-judicial" function. But per the Brennan Center's analysis of records provided pursuant to the Freedom of Information Act (FOIA), at least 74 OLC opinions, memoranda, or letters from 2002 to 2009 on some of the most important legal issues arising after 9/11—"including intelligence gathering and the detention and interrogation of suspected terrorists"—remain classified and

thus unavailable for public scrutiny. The Brennan Center also reports that between 1998 and 2003, at least one out of every five OLC opinions was classified. In some cases, OLC reports are not just withheld from the public; they're also withheld from Congress, including even the very Congressional committees with jurisdiction over the subject matter of the opinions. This practice—"unknown before the Reagan administration" and "rare before 9/11," according to the report—not only strips Congress of its oversight function, but also prevents Congress from stepping in when the executive branch misinterprets a law or decides that a law doesn't bind it.

- Information about the scope of government surveillance of U.S. persons under Section 702 of the 2008 FISA Amendments Act (FAA). The U.S. government relies upon Section 702 as the statutory basis for its PRISM and Upstream mass surveillance programs. These programs sweep up data on hundreds of millions of people who have no connection to terrorist investigations, including countless Americans. Indeed, a hearing last May confirmed that Congress has no idea how many Americans have been impacted by Section 702. That's not reassuring. This information should be disclosed to the public—and to Congress—since the proportionality of the government's activities is an important part of assessing their legality.
- Office of Inspector General reports related to national security and civil liberties. Various federal agencies have an Office of the Inspector General (OIG), designed to serve in an oversight capacity and reporting to both Congress and the agency head. These offices also issue reports relating to national security and civil liberties issues, but not all of these reports have been disclosed or released to the public. The public needs to know how federal agencies are interpreting and applying the law.

These are just a few of the discrete, practical actions we've specifically called for in our joint letter to the President. Obama should also brief both Congress and the Privacy and Civil Liberties Oversight Board (PCLOB) to help inform their oversight. He should direct a government-wide review of whether and how agencies are disposing of information about U.S. persons collected through surveillance.

And he should release guidance on how the government considers constitutional concerns surrounding "parallel construction," the law enforcement practice of laundering evidence to avoid disclosing the true source, such as a warrantless search conducted as part of a secret surveillance program.

Obama, It's Time

Although some sunlight has been shed on the government's telephone and Internet mass surveillance programs—thanks to the leaks of whistleblowers, including Edward Snowden, the work of investigative journalists, and statements by public officials—we are still largely in the dark regarding not only how these programs impact innocent people, but also about the constitutionally suspect legal analysis the government has relied upon to justify its warrantless collection of our communications records.

This pervasive secrecy is undermining our status as a truly democratic nation. As the Brennan Center notes, "[j]ust as secret law is not truly law, a democracy that relies on it is not truly a democracy." Obama has the opportunity to stand up for democratic principles by shedding light on how these programs operate—and he should take it.

EVALUATING THE AUTHOR'S ARGUMENTS:

In this viewpoint, Jamie Williams argues that secrecy is damaging the ideal of the United States as a democratic nation. Do you agree or disagree, and why?

Viewpoint 6

Both Republicans and Democrats Are Guilty When It Comes to Intelligence Matters

"Excessive domination by the political branches of government have long been recognized by intelligence scholars as the twin perils of spycraft."

Julian Sanchez

In the following excerpted viewpoint, Julian Sanchez demonstrates that both political parties in the United States play a role in the problems of intelligence. Sanchez points out that in some cases problems arise because individuals have attained too much power with little or no legal oversight. Other times problems develop as a result of partisan politics. In any case, those in power can learn valuable lessons from the past. Julian Sanchez is a senior fellow at the Cato Institute.

AS YOU READ, CONSIDER THE FOLLOWING QUESTIONS:

1. According to Sanchez, how did J. Edgar Hoover hold power in the FBI?
2. As stated by Sanchez, what was President Richard Nixon guilty of?
3. How are the actions of previous persons affecting President Trump's team according to the viewpoint?

"Republicans and Democrats Are Both Wrong about Leaks from Intelligence Agencies," by Julian Sanchez, Cato Institute, May 26, 2017. Reprinted by permission.

Among the myriad sideshow oddities of the Trump era: Republicans in Congress, as if suddenly awakening to the massive surveillance apparatus they spent the past 15 years constructing, belatedly echo civil liberties concerns they once reflexively ridiculed; they even threaten to curtail some Bush-era surveillance authorities. Meanwhile, many on the left grow positively giddy over leaked transcripts of Americans' National Security Agency-intercepted conversations, provided said Americans work for the Republican White House.

The facile, cynical read on this would be that the only bedrock principle in politics is tribal advantage—which is probably half the story. But seen through a more charitable lens, this recent inversion both obeys a shared underlying logic and reflects a common underlying confusion.

The underlying logic is this: Excessive autonomy from, and excessive domination by, the political branches of government have long been recognized by intelligence scholars as the twin perils of spycraft. Excessive autonomy gives rise to what we could dub the J. Edgar Hoover problem, after the legendary and infamous FBI director whose umbral half-century tenure saw the bureau run as a personal fiefdom, largely insulated from political accountability. The trove of embarrassing secrets—personal and political—about prominent Americans stored in Hoover's files gave his nominal overseers in Congress and the White House good reason to fear crossing him.

Problems on the Right, Problems on the Left

Concerns of this sort have traditionally been more prominent on the left, in no small part because of the long and ignominious history of intelligence abuses directed at that end of the political spectrum. More recently, the intelligence bureaucracy that conservative demonology now dubs the "deep state" was the subject of Tufts international relations scholar Michael Glennon's "National Security and Double Government" (later expanded into a book of the same name). Contemporary invocations of the concept routinely veer into the realm of conspiracy theory, but the core idea—that there is an entrenched national security establishment with significant power to

Your approval of the surveillance state might depend on whether your political party is in office.

advance its own aims, even in the face of opposition from the political branches—is neither novel nor fantastical.

Excessive subordination to the political branches, however, is no less dangerous. Call that the Richard Nixon problem, recalling how a Senate investigation concluded that the president had "authorized a program of wiretaps which produced for the White House purely political or personal information unrelated to national security." It is entirely too easy to imagine a political loyalist at the head of the FBI, directing the bureau to selectively investigate Fox News's villain of the day while turning a blind eye to potential misconduct by those close to the White House. This seems to be exactly what former director James Comey feared.

Because both poles represent genuine dangers, determining which is the more urgent risk ultimately comes down to a judgment call about which looms closer under present circumstances. So it's probably inevitable that your level of alarm depends on your assessment of the current president and his propensity to abuse power. The error partisans tend to make is to pretend that only the threat about which they're currently most concerned is real.

That's linked to another fundamental mistake by both sides: the tendency to use current partisan attitudes as the lens through which law-enforcement phenomena can be understood. When Comey recommended that no charges be filed against Hillary Clinton for mishandling classified information, Republicans blasted him for carrying water for Democrats. When Comey later informed members of Congress that the FBI was (briefly and without consequence, as it transpired) resurrecting the Clinton investigation, liberals accused him of deliberately seeking to throw the election to Donald Trump. Both accounts are mistaken. Whatever you think of Comey's judgment, the intelligence community and the people who staff it follow the institutional logic and interests of their agencies. That may mean that their actions overlap with the agenda of either party at any given time, but that agenda is rarely the driving force.

Cautious Ambivalence

The failure or refusal to understand this prevents partisans from comprehending what's going on when intelligence and politics parlously intersect. It also leads them to cheer or damn developments more wisely regarded with cautious ambivalence.

Consider a story broken by Reuters recently. Contrary to White House denials, it said, Trump campaign officials had numerous undisclosed contacts with the Russian government, both before and after the November election. Michael Flynn, the former national security adviser, and Russian Ambassador Sergey Kislyak "discussed establishing a back channel for communication between Trump and Russian President Vladimir Putin that could bypass the U.S. national security bureaucracy, which both sides considered hostile to improved relations."

Fast Fact

J. Edgar Hoover ran the FBI for nearly fifty years.

That account is ascribed to "four current U.S. officials," so it seems reasonable to infer that it was derived from intelligence intercepts of Kislyak and Flynn's conversations. It's not hard to imagine why intelligence officials might view the disclosure of such information as both legitimately in the public interest and, in the wake of Comey's dismissal, even necessary. One need not speculate about "Obama holdovers" (a phrase often deployed by conspiratorially minded commentators on the right as a synonym for "career intelligence professionals") dedicated to undermining the administration to explain such a leak. We had, after all, an incoming national security adviser—later revealed to have been acting as an unregistered paid agent of Turkey, as well as to have accepted undisclosed payments from Russian state media—collaborating with the ambassador of a country that had just meddled in a presidential election to avoid scrutiny by American intelligence agencies. With the administration taking drastic steps that appeared calculated to tamp down an investigation into the "made-up" question of collusion between the Trump campaign and Russia, intelligence officials with no particular partisan ax to grind might view going to the press (a felony, incidentally) as the only way to prevent facts with significant national security implications from vanishing down the memory hole.

Yet in addition to Nixon's "purely political" wiretaps, history provides numerous examples of intelligence abuses with origins in some inquiry with a plausibly legitimate national security purpose. (The FBI's notorious COINTELPRO operation, for instance, initially targeted radical groups advocating armed violence before metamorphosing into a campaign of harassment against peaceful left-leaning activists.) And it's probably impossible to know how any public-spirited motives for the latest Flynn disclosure might be colored by widely reported resentment within the FBI toward the dismissal of a well-loved director, in a peremptory manner that many viewed as an insult. This leak ought, then, to give even the administration's fiercest critics pause.

If we take it at face value (leaving aside whether that's proper), the Flynn intercept reveals a president-elect apparently worried that his foreign policy would be undermined by his own government's intelligence agencies. It would be easier to dismiss that fear as yet another fit of Trumpian paranoia if it didn't seem like we were learning about that conversation from wiretaps.

Progressives who've recently learned to stop worrying and love the surveillance state should think hard about the precedent such leaks set—and the implicit message they send to political actors—even if any particular instance can be justified as serving the public interest. The leaks may not be, as conservative media would have it, the only real scandal, but nobody should be too enthusiastic about the prospect of living in a country where officials who antagonize spy agencies find their telephone conversations quoted in news headlines.

Trump fans, meanwhile, should not make the mistake of thinking that the only reason to worry about the deep state is that it remains Barack Obama's deep state. The most effective bulwark against abuse of the intelligence community's power is not the bodies charged with overseeing the spy agencies—all ultimately depend on candor and disclosure from the agencies themselves—but the fragile culture of restraint that fitfully emerged in the aftermath of the scandals of the 1960s and '70s. Whatever remains of that culture 16 years into the war on terrorism, hollowing out the intelligence bureaucracy to make room for appointees selected for their personal loyalty to Trump would probably finish it off.

EVALUATING THE AUTHOR'S ARGUMENTS:

In this viewpoint, Julian Sanchez finds fault with both Republicans and Democrats in the issues of classified information and government secrets. In view of the divided opinions of many Americans, how does this affect the country?

Chapter 2

How Does Classified Intelligence Affect the United States?

Leaking classified information is either heroic or treasonous, depending on your perspective.

Viewpoint 1

Disclosure or Leaking of Classified Information Is Damaging

"At this moment we are debating in ways we never have before issues surrounding the revelation of classified information."

Peter Hoekstra

In the following viewpoint, Peter Hoekstra defines and analyzes how classified information is leaked. Beginning with the example of Valerie Plame, a CIA covert officer whose identity was leaked in a 2003 government scandal, Hoekstra argues that leaks cause a multitude of problems that can result in distrust and genuine danger. The author provides examples that illustrate his contentions, underscoring the complexity of this issue. Peter Hoekstra is a former member of the United States House of Representatives and former Chairman of the House Intelligence Committee.

AS YOU READ, CONSIDER THE FOLLOWING QUESTIONS:

1. What are the three categories of intelligence leaks reported by Peter Hoekstra?
2. According to Hoekstra, how do intelligence leaks help US enemies?
3. Why is it so difficult to prosecute leaking of information as stated by the author?

"Secrets and Leaks: The Costs and Consequences for National Security," by Peter Hoekstra, The Heritage Foundation, July 29, 2005. Reprinted by permission.

Unauthorized leaks can result in irreparable damage to the intelligence community.

The issue of leaks has been front and center in the news, in case some of you hadn't noticed. And I'm not just talking about Valerie Plame. While much has been made of the revelation of her name, it is not my intention to rehash or debate the particulars of that case today. In due time, the Independent Counsel will release his report, and all the facts of the situation will be made clear.

But if you cut through all the partisan rhetoric surrounding this case, it does help to bring the issue of leaks to the forefront. At this moment we are debating in ways we never have before issues surrounding the revelation of classified information. There is a bill before the Senate to create a media shield law, there are discussions on the classification process and whether too much information is being classified, and most importantly, we are debating the public's right to know more about the activities of their government.

At the outset, I want to make it clear that I am a firm believer in representative government and the people's right to know. As such, I am committed to doing more of the Intelligence Committee's hearings in public and to reviewing the issue of how much the government classifies.

But today, my scope is more narrowly focused on the issue of leaks of classified information, which I break into three different categories: accidental, deliberate and espionage-related.

The Damage Brought on by Leaks

It has become all too common—almost second nature—for people in Washington to leak information. Policymakers may leak for any number of reasons, such as to bring attention to a good news story or discredit a bad story. They may also leak information to gauge public interest on a new policy or issue. But some seemingly leak just because they can.

These are the people, and especially those that have access to classified information, that we need to worry about.

On the walls of the Intelligence Committee are framed posters from World War II that remind of the dangers of leaks. "LOOSE LIPS MIGHT SINK SHIPS," says one poster that was originally sponsored by the House of Seagram's. Another poster shows a ship in flames, its crew bobbing in the water and on lifeboats with the statement, "A CARELESS WORD … A NEEDLESS SINKING." The ghosts of leaks past serve as potent reminders for us of the dangers of leaks today.

Each year, countless unauthorized leaks cause severe damage to our intelligence activities and expose our capabilities. The fact of the matter is, some of the worst damage done to our intelligence community has come not from penetration by spies, but from unauthorized leaks by those with access to classified information.

Were it not for a leak, there is a chance we could have brought Usama bin Laden to justice by now and have a better understanding of the al-Qaida operation. Several years ago, highly sensitive information was disclosed regarding the intelligence communities' ability to collect information on bin Laden. Reportedly as a result, bin Laden changed his methods of operation, and we lost a valuable means of understanding al-Qaida's movements and future plans.

Now I realize there may be times when a person entrusted with classified information makes an unintentional disclosure. But, the Intelligence Community must be prepared to deal with these instances because all classified leaks can be dangerous.

When it comes to deliberate disclosures of classified information, however, we must create a culture within the Intelligence Community where zero tolerance is the norm. People entrusted with a security clearance must realize their clearance is not a right, it is a privilege, and it must be treated as such. Just because a person has a security clearance does not give them the authority to exercise leadership in determining what should and should not be classified.

> **Fast Fact**
>
> **During the presidency of Richard Nixon, wiretaps were used on White House staff to uncover leaks of classified information.**

Earlier this year, for example, the Department of Justice arrested Lawrence Franklin, a Pentagon defense analyst, for removing 83 documents from the Pentagon. Amazingly, this is not the first time Mr. Franklin was accused of compromising classified information, but his clearances were never suspended or revoked. We have to ask, did the previous leniency shown to Mr. Franklin contribute to his decision to go even further in revealing classified information? And then we should be outraged. It is painfully obvious we must change the culture within the Intelligence Community.

The inability to protect our sources and methods from intentional leaks causes substantial damage to our intelligence services and national security.

After 9/11, the intelligence community was blamed for not sharing information or translating pieces of intelligence in a timely manner to prevent the attacks from occurring. People should be equally upset that there are individuals who deliberately leak classified information. If that information gets into the hands of our enemies it can help them plan future attacks.

We know the enemy pays very close attention to open-source materials, like U.S. newspapers and the Internet, in order to gain a better understanding of our objectives and capabilities.

A June 2002 memo from the CIA discusses the damage caused when classified information is reported in the media. It reads in part, "Information obtained from captured detainees has revealed that al-Qaida operatives are extremely security-conscious and have altered their practices in response to what they have learned from the press about our capabilities. A growing body of reporting indicates that al-Qaida planners have learned much about our counter-terrorist capabilities from U.S. and foreign media." By combining traditional open source materials with leaked classified materials our opponents have gained powerful insights into what our plans, capabilities and intentions are.

Damage Abroad

We also know that unauthorized leaks put strains on our relationships with foreign intelligence services. Despite being the best at what we do, it is impossible to collect every piece of intelligence in every corner of the world. As a result, we count on foreign intelligence services to help fill-in the gaps.

Unauthorized leaks could have a significant impact on whether foreign governments continue to share critical information with our intelligence agencies. And quite frankly, I cannot blame them.

The reality is, many foreign leaders and their governments provide us with valuable help in the war on terror, but they do so at tremendous political peril. If the United States cannot promise to protect classified information and where we got it from, why should we expect these leaders, or even our overt allies, to be willing to share their information?

Information sharing with foreign intelligence services will play a significant role in our intelligence collection capabilities in the future. The loss of foreign partners would undoubtedly create overwhelming gaps in our ability to collect good intelligence around the globe.

Some of you may have seen an article from a few weeks ago that discussed possible coordination between the U.S., France and other governments in the war on terror. While I understand the public has a certain interest in knowing what the government is doing to protect them, we have to ask, where is the balance. What was the benefit of publishing that story?

Reports that discuss sensitive partnerships, whether accurate or not, hinder our abilities to work with our friends on intelligence activities. Some foreign nations work with our agencies because it is not widely known that they are doing it. That secrecy is important for future operations.

The Commission on Weapons of Mass Destruction reports the Intelligence Community seriously misjudged the status of Iraq's biological weapons program in the 2002 National Intelligence Estimate and other pre-war intelligence products. The primary reason for this misjudgment was the Intelligence Community's heavy reliance on a source-codenamed "Curveball"-whose information later proved to be unreliable.

This misjudgment could have been avoided if we were able to receive key information from our allies. The decision by a foreign intelligence service not to share a critical source seriously undermined our ability to assess his credibility. Despite numerous requests by the CIA, the foreign government refused to provide us direct access to Curveball because of past leaks from within our government.

The classified annex to the Silberman-Robb Report on Weapons of Mass Destruction discusses numerous cases over the past several years that have cost American taxpayers plenty, not to mention the harm caused by the exposure of our assets, methods and capabilities. Because it is classified I cannot elaborate further, but you do not need to read a classified annex to get a sense of the frequency that leaks occur and the damage they cause. I am confident the terrorists are not reading the classified annex to get their information.

How to Stop It?

Leaking sensitive information is like giving the enemy our playbook. In 2002 a newspaper obtained classified information about top-secret war plans leading up to the invasion in Iraq. Then last week, there were wire service stories on possible American and British plans to bring troops home by the end of the year. Whether accurate or not, these types of stories put our operational capabilities at risk and allow the enemy to manipulate the information for possible use against our brave men and women in uniform.

How much damage has to be done before people finally say enough is enough? We must get serious about re-evaluating leaks and our response to them.

The primary question is how do we do that?

If you talk to the different agencies, especially the Justice Department, they will tell you that leaks occur so frequently because it is extremely difficult to identify who leaked the information and then obtain a successful prosecution.

This is a problem I expect to get worse, not better, as we continue to press for increased information sharing community-wide. Agencies do not have the resources to spend months investigating a case when there is no way to narrow down the list of people who had access to the information. Simply put, more people have access to more information than ever before, and while it is necessary, it makes investigating leaks even that more difficult.

We also have to contend with the fact that there is no comprehensive statute that provides criminal penalties for the unauthorized disclosure of classified information regardless of the type of information or the recipient involved.

As a result, the Department of Justice is left with a "patchwork" of statutes to go after those who leak. Subsequently, there has only been one prosecution for non-espionage disclosure of classified information in the last 50 years. In the case of *United States v. Morrison*, the courts found the defendant guilty of providing classified information to Jane's Defense.

And President Clinton pardoned Morison before he left office.

We need to bring new energy to this debate. The threat leaks pose to our national security is alarming, and it is imperative we do more to protect our national secrets.

Whether people deliberately leak information or they don't realize the information they are discussing is classified, the fact that leaks continue is evidence that people in the intelligence community are not being properly educated on the importance of protecting our secrets.

The community, upon direction from the DNI, should implement a community-wide campaign to educate individuals about their legal obligations and possible penalties for failing to safeguard intelligence information.

In addition, we need to give the Department of Justice all the tools it needs to identify and prosecute individuals who deliberately share classified intelligence. The time has come for a comprehensive law that will make it easier for the government to prosecute wrongdoers and increase the penalties, which hopefully will act as a deterrent for people thinking about disclosing information.

In the coming months, I intend to hold a round of hearings on this issue and invite key officials from Justice, CIA and the Defense Department, among others, to testify on ways the Intelligence Community can do more to prevent leaks.

If they agree to attend, I would also like to invite members of the press to testify before the committee. Journalists provide an important service to the American people, but they can also play a key role in preserving our national security.

The recent interest in leaks has inspired some Members of Congress to introduce a Media Shield Law, which would protect journalists from disclosing their sources. While I believe this may be permissible in most cases, this bill could have serious implications if passed without exceptions when our national security is at risk.

There needs to be a balance between protecting journalists and protecting national security. I believe we can find that balance.

The Silberman-Robb Commission recognized "the enormous difficulty of this seemingly intractable problem" and concluded that "the long-standing defeatism that has paralyzed action on the topic of leaks is understandable but unwarranted."

I too share that assessment, and I look forward to a full and vigorous debate on this issue.

EVALUATING THE AUTHOR'S ARGUMENTS:

In this viewpoint, Peter Hoekstra analyzes several examples of how leaking of intelligence information does damage to the United States. Using one of his examples, expand upon the idea that leaking of information does damage to US foreign relations.

Viewpoint 2

The President May Have Jeopardized Intelligence Efforts

"Revealing classified information at this level is extremely dangerous and puts at risk the lives of Americans and those who gather intelligence for our country."

Jessica Taylor

In the following viewpoint, Jessica Taylor cites news sources that have uncovered details of President Donald Trump's possible unveiling of classified information to Russian officials. The issue of collusion with the Russians has dogged Trump's presidency almost from the onset. Taylor highlights the important issues of the story, including President Trump's boasting of his daily briefings on intelligence matters, the effort by senior White House members to contain the damage, and the response by several government officials. Jessica Taylor is the digital political reporter for National Public Radio.

AS YOU READ, CONSIDER THE FOLLOWING QUESTIONS:

1. According to Taylor, what is code-word information?
2. As stated in the viewpoint, is Trump's disclosure of information illegal?
3. Do the reactions by politicians as revealed by the author seem partisan?

The president has the power to declassify any information, but did Donald Trump misstep when he met with top Russian officials in the Oval Office?

President Trump revealed "highly classified information" to two top Russian officials during a controversial Oval Office meeting last week, according to a report from *The Washington Post.*

The Post, citing current and former U.S. officials, reported Monday evening that the information relayed by the president to Russian Foreign Minister Sergey Lavrov and Ambassador Sergey Kislyak "jeopardized a critical source of intelligence" on ISIS:

> *The partner had not given the United States permission to share the material with Russia, and officials said Trump's decision to do so endangers cooperation from an ally that has access to the inner workings of the Islamic State. After Trump's meeting, senior White House officials took steps to contain the damage, placing calls to the CIA and the National Security Agency.*
>
> *"This is code-word information," said a U.S. official familiar with the matter, using terminology that refers to one of the highest classification levels used by American spy agencies. Trump "revealed more information to the Russian ambassador than we have shared with our own allies."*

Trump also reportedly boasted to the Russians about the intelligence he was receiving, telling the two men, "I get great intel. I have people brief me on great intel every day":

> *Trump went on to discuss aspects of the threat that the United States learned only through the espionage capabilities of a key partner. He did not reveal the specific intelligence-gathering method, but he described how the Islamic State was pursuing elements of a specific plot and how much harm such an attack could cause under varying circumstances. Most alarmingly, officials said, Trump revealed the city in the Islamic State's territory where the U.S. intelligence partner detected the threat.*
>
> The Washington Post *is withholding most plot details, including the name of the city, at the urging of officials who warned that revealing them would jeopardize important intelligence capabilities.*

Greg Miller, one of *The Post* reporters who broke the story, told NPR's Ari Shapiro on *All Things Considered* that by sharing the information from another country, it could damage future intelligence gathering and U.S. relations with other partners.

"This is not intelligence that the United States gathered or owned. It wasn't up to the United States to share, and so doing so really jeopardizes that relationship. It potentially damages trust that's critical in these kinds of arrangements. And I think that's one of the really big worries here," Miller told NPR. "And in this case it's important, because this is apparently an ongoing stream of intelligence into Islamic State plotting. I mean, what could be more important?"

BuzzFeed also confirmed *The Post*'s report, with one U.S. official saying that the disclosures from the president to the Russians were "far worse than what has already been reported."

The New York Times also noted that "Trump's disclosure does not appear to have been illegal—the president has the power to declassify almost anything. But sharing the information without the express permission of the ally who provided it represented a major breach of espionage etiquette and could jeopardize a crucial intelligence-sharing relationship."

Trump's meeting with the Russians came last Wednesday, the day after he fired FBI Director James Comey, who was overseeing an investigation into Russian meddling in the U.S. elections and possible ties between the Trump campaign and Russia.

FAST FACT

Code word information is highly classified and has a higher secrecy status than information classified as Top Secret.

The visit was fraught with bad optics, and Kislyak's attendance—only confirmed by photos from Russian state media—was especially notable because he has been at the center of many of the Trump administration's controversies involving Russia. Only a Russian Foreign Ministry photographer was allowed in to document the meeting; no U.S. media were allowed.

Trump's first national security adviser, Michael Flynn, was forced to resign after just over three weeks on the job after it was revealed he had discussed Russian sanctions with Kislyak and then subsequently misled Vice President Pence about those conversations. Attorney General Jeff Sessions was forced to recuse himself from any involvement in the FBI's investigations into Russia after it was revealed that he twice met with Kislyak, despite testifying during his confirmation hearing that he had had no contact with Russian officials.

Monday's reports of Trump revealing classified information to the Russians come just ahead of his first foreign trip as president. He's set to depart on Friday, traveling to Saudi Arabia, Israel and the Vatican, then attending a NATO meeting in Brussels, Belgium, and a G7 meeting in Italy.

National Security Adviser H.R. McMaster told reporters outside the White House that the "story that came out tonight, as reported, is false."

"At no time were intelligence sources or methods discussed, and the president did not disclose any military operations that were not already publicly known," McMaster said. However, *The Post* story and other subsequent reports didn't say that it was sources, methods or military operations discussed, but simply classified information.

"I was in the room, and it didn't happen," McMaster said at the end of his abrupt statement. He departed without taking questions.

"During President Trump's meeting with Foreign Minister Lavrov, a broad range of subjects were discussed among which were common efforts and threats regarding counter-terrorism," Secretary of State Rex Tillerson said in a statement. "During that exchange the nature of specific threats were discussed, but they did not discuss sources, methods or military operations."

Senate Foreign Relations Committee Chairman Bob Corker, R-Tenn., said in a statement that, "I want to learn more about what occurred and what was shared, but if true, this report is troubling." Corker told *Bloomberg News* that the White House was "in a downward spiral right now and they've got to figure out a way to come to grips with all that's happening."

Senate Intelligence Committee Vice Chairman Mark Warner, D-Va., said that if *The Washington Post*'s report was true, it was "inexcusable."

Eliot Cohen, a former counselor to Secretary of State Condoleezza Rice under President George W. Bush, said on Twitter that if Trump had given the classified material to the Russians deliberately, "it would be treason."

House Minority Leader Nancy Pelosi, D-Calif., said in a statement that Congress "must be given a full briefing on the extent of the damage President Trump has done in compromising highly classified code-word intelligence to the Russians."

"Even if President Trump unwittingly blew a highly classified code-word source to the Russians, that would be dangerous enough," Pelosi said. "If the President outed a highly classified code-word source intentionally, that would be even more dangerous."

Senate Minority Leader Chuck Schumer, D-N.Y., echoed those sentiments and called on the president to provide a "full explanation" to Congress, the intelligence community and the public.

"If the report is true, it is very disturbing," Schumer said. "Revealing classified information at this level is extremely dangerous and puts at risk the lives of Americans and those who gather intelligence for our country."

Throughout the campaign, Trump repeatedly criticized his Democratic opponent, former Secretary of State Hillary Clinton, over her mishandling of classified information on her private email server. At his rallies, the crowd frequently chanted "Lock her up!"

House Speaker Paul Ryan said back in July, with regard to Clinton's emails, that people who are "extremely careless" with classified information no longer should have access to it.

On Monday, Ryan spokesman Doug Andres said that, "We have no way to know what was said, but protecting our nation's secrets is paramount. The speaker hopes for a full explanation of the facts from the administration."

EVALUATING THE AUTHOR'S ARGUMENTS:

In this viewpoint, Jessica Taylor provides information surrounding the question whether President Trump has given classified intelligence to the Russians. Do you think that the president is guilty of this charge? Defend your stance with statements from this viewpoint and explain the ramifications this would have on US security.

Viewpoint 3

Americans Suffer When Phone and Internet Communications Are Intercepted

"All of these surveillance activities are in violation of the privacy safeguards established by Congress and the US Constitution."

The Electronic Frontier Foundation

In the following viewpoint, the Electronic Frontier Foundation (EFF) accuses government agencies of violating the privacy of average American citizens. The basis of the accusations are the 2005 revelations that the US government had been conducting mass surveillance of Americans' communications since 2001, and that telecom giants were aiding in this surveillance. The EFF presents several incidents where this has occurred. The EFF is a nonprofit organization that defends civil liberties in the digital world.

AS YOU READ, CONSIDER THE FOLLOWING QUESTIONS:

1. According to the EFF, when did the collection of information begin?
2. How is information collected for the NSA as stated by the author?
3. Which constitutional amendment is being used to block access according to this viewpoint?

"NSA Spying", The Electronic Frontier Foundation. https://www.eff.org/nsa-spying.

The US government, with assistance from major telecommunications carriers including AT&T, has engaged in massive, illegal dragnet surveillance of the domestic communications and communications records of millions of ordinary Americans since at least 2001. Since this was first reported on by the press and discovered by the public in late 2005, EFF has been at the forefront of the effort to stop it and bring government surveillance programs back within the law and the Constitution.

History of NSA Spying Information since 2005

News reports in December 2005 first revealed that the National Security Agency (NSA) has been intercepting Americans' phone calls and Internet communications. Those news reports, combined with a *USA Today* story in May 2006 and the statements of several members of Congress, revealed that the NSA is also receiving wholesale copies of American's telephone and other communications records. All of these surveillance activities are in violation of the privacy safeguards established by Congress and the US Constitution.

In early 2006, EFF obtained whistleblower evidence from former AT&T technician Mark Klein showing that AT&T is cooperating with the illegal surveillance. The undisputed documents show that AT&T installed a fiberoptic splitter at its facility at 611 Folsom Street in San Francisco that makes copies of all emails web browsing and other Internet traffic to and from AT&T customers and provides those copies to the NSA. This copying includes both domestic and international Internet activities of AT&T customers. As one expert observed, "this isn't a wiretap, it's a country-tap."

Secret government documents, published by the media in 2013, confirm the NSA obtains full copies of everything that is carried along major domestic fiber optic cable networks. In June 2013, the media, led by the *Guardian* and *Washington Post* started publishing a series of articles, along with full government documents, that have confirmed much of what was reported in 2005 and 2006 and then some. The reports showed-and the government later admitted—that the government is mass collecting phone metadata of all US customers under the guise of the Patriot Act. Moreover, the media reports confirm that the government is collecting and analyzing the content

Americans were shocked to learn that the government had been spying on them, with the help of their telecommunications providers.

of communications of foreigners talking to persons inside the United States, as well as collecting much more, without a probable cause warrant. Finally, the media reports confirm the "upstream" collection off of the fiberoptic cables that Mr. Klein first revealed in 2006.

EFF Fights Back in the Courts

EFF is fighting these illegal activities in the courts. Currently, EFF is representing victims of the illegal surveillance program in Jewel v. NSA, a lawsuit filed in September 2008 seeking to stop the warrantless wiretapping and hold the government and government officials behind the program accountable. In July 2013, a federal judge ruled that the government could not rely on the controversial "state secrets" privilege to block our challenge to the constitutionality of the program. On February 10, 2015, however, the court granted summary judgment to the government on the Plaintiffs' allegations of Fourth Amendment violations based on the NSA's copying of Internet traffic from the Internet backbone. The court ruled that the publicly available information did not paint a complete picture of how the NSA collects Internet traffic, so the court could not rule on the program without looking at information that could constitute "state secrets." The court did not rule that the NSA's activities are legal, nor did it rule on the other claims in Jewel, and the case will go forward on those claims. This case is being heard in conjunction with *Shubert v. Obama*, which raises similar claims.

Fast Fact

In a 2015 Pew survey, 57 percent of Americans say it is unacceptable to monitor communications from American citizens.

In July, 2013, EFF filed another lawsuit, *First Unitarian v. NSA*, based on the recently published FISA court order demanding Verizon turn over all customer phone records including who is talking to whom, when and for how long—to the NSA. This so-called "meta-data," especially when collected in bulk and aggregated, allows the government to track the associations of various political and religious organizations. The Director of National Intelligence has since confirmed that the collection of Verizon call records is part of a broader program.

In addition to making the same arguments we made in Jewel, we argue in First Unitarian that this type of collection violates the First Amendment right to association. Previously, in *Hepting v. AT&T*, EFF filed the first case against a cooperating telecom for violating its customers' privacy. After Congress expressly intervened and passed the FISA Amendments Act to allow the Executive to require dismissal of the case, *Hepting* was ultimately dismissed by the US Supreme Court.

In September of 2014, EFF, along with the American Civil Liberties Union (ACLU) and the American Civil Liberties Union of Idaho, joined the legal team for Anna Smith, an Idaho emergency neonatal nurse, in her challenge of the government's bulk collection of the telephone records of millions of innocent Americans. In *Smith v. Obama*, we are arguing the program violated her Fourth Amendment rights by collecting a wealth of detail about her familial, political, professional, religious and intimate associations. In particular, we focus on challenging the applicability of the so-called "third party doctrine," the idea that people have no expectation of privacy in information they entrust to others.

EVALUATING THE AUTHOR'S ARGUMENTS:

In this viewpoint, the Electronic Frontier Foundation argues that the government's program of data and phone record collection is illegal, even if the intention is to protect US citizens. Do you agree or disagree? Justify your opinion.

Viewpoint 4

Why Keep the US Public in the Dark About Surveillance?

"The FBI has gone to great lengths to keep this technology secret, even going as far as refusing to tell judges its full range of capabilities."

Parker Higgins and Trevor Timm

In the following viewpoint, Parker Higgins and Trevor Timm argue that information about US government surveillance techniques is being kept away from the American public. Higgins and Timm present evidence about secret surveillance that the FBI and local law enforcement use. Higgins and Timm argue that to inform the public would cause no harm, and in fact it is well within the rights of citizens to know. Higgins is director of special projects at Freedom of the Press Foundation and former directory of copyright activism at Electronic Frontier Foundation. Timm is co-founder and executive director at Freedom of the Press Foundation and a columnist for *The Guardian*.

AS YOU READ, CONSIDER THE FOLLOWING QUESTIONS:

1. How does the FBI keep information from the public according to Higgins and Timm?
2. What are three types of surveillance tools according to the authors?
3. As stated in the viewpoint, what role does the public play in law enforcement?

"What the FBI Doesn't Want You To Know About Its 'Secret' Surveillance Techniques," by Parker Higgins and Trevor Timm, The Electronic Frontier Foundation, January 17, 2013. https://www.eff.org/deeplinks/2013/01/what-fbi-doesnt-want-you-know-about-its-surveillance-techniques.

Every time we use our phones the government could be tracking us.

The FBI had to rewrite the book on its domestic surveillance activities in the wake of last January's landmark Supreme Court decision in *United States v. Jones*. In *Jones*, a unanimous court held that federal agents must get a warrant to attach a GPS device to a car to track a suspect for long periods of time. But if you want to see the two memos describing how the FBI has reacted to Jones—and the new surveillance techniques the FBI is using beyond GPS trackers—you're out of luck. The FBI says that information is "private and confidential."

Yes, now that the Supreme Court ruled the government must get a warrant to use its previous go-to surveillance technique, it has now apparently decided that it's easier to just keep everything secret. The ACLU requested the memos under the Freedom of Information Act and the FBI redacted them almost entirely.

Though the FBI won't release the memos, we do have some information from other sources on the surveillance techniques federal agents are already using. And for the most part the FBI contends they do not need a warrant, and one wonders, given the public nature of this information, why they are officially claiming its "secret."

FAST FACT

Many law enforcement agencies will not acknowledge that they either own or use stingray tracking devices.

Cell Phone Data Requests

Tellingly, in *U.S. v. Jones*, after the US government lost its case in the Supreme Court with the GPS device, it went right back to the district court and asserted it could get Jones' cell phone site location data without a warrant. EFF has long argued cell location data, which can map your precise location for days or weeks at a time, is highly personal, and should require a warrant from a judge.

In July 2012, the *New York Times* reported that federal, state, and local law enforcement officials had requested all kinds of cell phone data, including mappings of suspects' locations, a staggering 1.3 million times in the previous year. Worse, the real number was "almost certainly much higher" given they often request multiple people's data with one request. The FBI also employs highly controversial "tower dumps" where they get the location information on *everyone* within a particular radius, potentially violating the privacy of thousands of innocent people with one request.

Stingray Interceptors

In late 2012, we reported on the secretive new device the FBI has been increasingly using for surveillance known as a IMSI catcher, or "Stingray." A Stingray acts as a fake cell phone tower and locks onto all devices in a certain area to find a cell phone's location, or perhaps even intercept phone calls and texts. Given it potentially sucks up thousands of innocent persons' data, we called it an "unconstitutional, all you can eat data buffet."

The FBI has gone to great lengths to keep this technology secret, even going as far as refusing to tell judges its full range of capabilities. Recently, documents obtained by EPIC Privacy through a FOIA request shed more light on the devices.

License Plate Readers

In cities across the country, local police departments and other law enforcement agencies are installing automated license plate readers that create databases of location information about individual cars (and their drivers). These readers can be mounted by the side of a busy road, scanning every car that rolls by, or on the dash of a police car, allowing officers to drive through and scan all the plates in a parking lot.

In Washington, D.C., nearly every block is captured by one of the more than 250 cameras scanning over 1,800 images per minute. In Los Angeles, more than two dozen different law enforcement agencies operate license plate readers to collect over 160 million data points. This surveillance is untargeted, recording the movements of any car passes by. In cities that have become partners in the FBI's Joint Terrorism Task Force, or have entered into another data-sharing agreement, this location information is at the fingertips of those federal agents.

Drone Authorization

On top of all this, the FBI is one of just a few dozen public agencies that has an authorization to fly a drone in the U.S. There is no evidence at this time that they are actively pursuing or using a specific device. But we do know that other branches of the federal government, namely the Department of Homeland Security (DHS), are conducting drone surveillance along the U.S. border, and have at least occasionally loaned these capabilities to other departments. EFF has sued DHS for more information about that program, but in the meantime, as with the redacted documents, information about their use in surveillance remains frustratingly opaque.

Secret Law

This is just the latest example of the Obama administration trying to interpret public laws in secret without adequately informing its citizens. Currently, EFF is suing the government for its secret interpretation of the Patriot Act Section 215, and for secret FISA court opinions that could shed light on the NSA warrantless wiretapping program. In addition, the ACLU has sued the Obama administration for its legal opinion stating it can kill US citizens overseas, away from the battlefield.

Of course, law enforcement needs the ability to conduct investigations. But explaining to the public how it *generally* conducts surveillance puts no one in danger, and compromises no investigations. After all, criminals have known the FBI has been able to wiretap phones with a warrant for decades and it hasn't stopped them from using wiretaps to catch them.

This information is vital to know if law enforcement is complying with the law and constitution. As we've seen with GPS devices, and we are now seeing with cell phone tracking and the use of Stingrays, law enforcement will push the limits of their authority—and sometimes overstep it—if they are not kept in check by an informed public.

EVALUATING THE AUTHORS' ARGUMENTS:

In this viewpoint, Parker Higgins and Trevor Timm analyze the surveillance tools used by government and local law enforcement. Higgins and Timm provide evidence to show that the agencies believe in using the surveillance, thereby gaining data. Do you agree with the law enforcement agencies that this must be kept secret? What could be the potential problems?

Chapter 3

Can Anything Be Done to Prevent Leaks of Classified Intelligence?

Now that the cat is out of the bag, can we put it back in?

Viewpoint 1

What Happens When Classified Intelligence Is Accidentally Leaked?

"The consequences of Trump's disclosure are both immediate and long-term."

Aaron Rupar

In the following viewpoint, Aaron Rupar analyzes an incident of accidental disclosure of intelligence to argue the importance of security on foreign relations. Rupar presents evidence to suggest that President Trump relayed partial bits of classified information to unauthorized Russian diplomats without first consulting the source of the information, which was Israel intelligence. While Trump's leak may be a result of the president's lack of understanding of the situation, rather than any sinister motives, the potential damage is done. Rupar's analysis also provides insight into future consequences of this disclosure. Aaron Rupar is a journalist and editor for ThinkProgress.

"OOPS: Trump accidentally confirms source of classified intel he gave to Russians," by Aaron Rupar, May 22, 2017. This material was created by Think Progress (thinkprogress.org). Reprinted by permission.

AS YOU READ, CONSIDER THE FOLLOWING QUESTIONS:

1. According to the viewpoint, does the Israeli Prime Minister at first seem concerned?
2. What role do Trump's advisors play in this incident as stated by Rupar?
3. What is different between the US and Israel according to the author?

During a photo opportunity with President Trump on Monday, Israeli Prime Minister Benjamin Netanyahu was asked if he's concerned about Trump sharing highly sensitive counterterrorism intelligence with Russian officials on May 10—information that reportedly came from an Israeli source.

Trump responded by telling reporters that he never mentioned the word "Israel" during that meeting with Russian foreign minister Sergey Lavrov and ambassador to the U.S. Sergey Kislyak.

"Just so you understand—I never mentioned the word or the name 'Israel,'" Trump said. "I never mentioned it during that conversation."

Gesturing to reporters, Trump added, "They were all saying I did. So you had another story wrong. Never mentioned the word 'Israel.'"

"Intelligence cooperation is terrific," Netanyahu said.

The details Trump shared about an ISIS plot to use an explosive tucked inside a laptop computer to bring down a U.S.-bound airplane were quickly traced back to an Israeli source. But before Trump's comments on Monday, administration officials hadn't publicly said anything about it, nor had they confirmed that the intelligence came from Israel.

During a news conference last week, National Security Adviser H.R. McMaster didn't deny that Trump shared classified information with the Russians, but said Trump "wasn't even aware of where that information came from."

Trump's comments on Monday also misrepresented mainstream media reports about his disclosure, none of which claimed he mentioned Israel by name during his meeting with the Russian diplomats.

Israel's prime minister Benjamin Netanyahu answered questions with President Trump.

The consequences of Trump's disclosure are both immediate and long-term. ABC, citing current and former U.S. officials, reported that Trump's actions endangered the life of a spy placed by Israel inside ISIS. Matt Olsen, the former Director of the National Counterterrorism Center, told ABC that "the real risk is not just this source…but future sources of information about plots against us."

On Friday, *Foreign Policy*, citing an unnamed Israeli intelligence officer, reported that Israel officials "are angry and alarmed" by the disclosure.

"The revelation that sensitive information may have been passed to Russia, a partner to Iran, was particularly concerning," *Foreign Policy* added. "Israel has become increasingly anxious about Russia's military cooperation with Iran in support of the Syrian regime and its growing cyberwarfare capabilities… In Israel, there is fear the compromise of intelligence could damage the country's interests and even jeopardize lives, the official said."

Similarly, two Israeli intelligence officials told *BuzzFeed* that Trump's disclosure was Israel's "worst fears confirmed."

"We have an arrangement with America which is unique to the world of intelligence sharing. We do not have this relationship with any other country," an anonymous Israeli official said, according to BuzzFeed. "There is a special understanding of security cooperation between our countries… To know that this intelligence is shared with others, without our prior knowledge? That is, for us, our worst fears confirmed."

Although Israelis aren't happy about Trump's conduct, Secretary of State Rex Tillerson said earlier Monday that no apology will be forthcoming.

FAST FACT

Israel is a country in the Middle East and an important ally of the United States.

"I don't know that there's anything to apologize for," Tillerson told reporters on Air Force One. "To the extent the Israelis have any questions, or clarification, I'm sure we're happy to provide that."

While Trump's comments brought renewed focus to the revelation that Trump took the unusual step of sharing highly sensitive intelligence with Russia on May 10, that development was overshadowed over the weekend by another bombshell report about what Trump told Russian officials during that Oval Office rendezvous.

On Friday, the *New York Times* reported that Trump told the top Russian diplomats that his move to fire FBI Director James Comey amid an ongoing FBI investigation into his campaign's links with Russia relied "great pressure" on him.

"I just fired the head of the FBI. He was crazy, a real nut job," Trump told Lavrov and Kislyak, according to a document read to Times reporters by an anonymous source. "I faced great pressure because of Russia. That's taken off."

The White House didn't dispute that Trump in fact said those words, which seem to confirm he fired Comey to obstruct an ongoing investigation into his campaign.

EVALUATING THE AUTHOR'S ARGUMENTS:

In this viewpoint, Aaron Rupar reports on an incident of apparent accidental disclosure of classified intelligence. Do you agree that the disclosure was accidental? Back up your opinion with evidence from the viewpoint.

Viewpoint 2

Too Much Classified Intelligence Is Leaked by the Media

"News outlets regularly published 'disastrous' stories which damaged US national security and exposed the involvement of US partners."

Marc A. Thiessen

In the following viewpoint, Marc A. Thiessen argues that the media is not innocent when it comes to intelligence leaks, and that they should take more accountability for their practices. Media outlets were outraged when reports surfaced that President Trump revealed classified information to the Russians. Thiessen contends that if this did happen it would be terribly unfortunate but also implies that the media's reaction is disingenuous since classified information was repeatedly leaked during the administration of President Obama. Marc A. Thiessen is a senior fellow at AEI, the American Enterprise Institute.

AS YOU READ, CONSIDER THE FOLLOWING QUESTIONS:

1. According to this viewpoint, does Thiessen agree that disclosure of intelligence is harmful?
2. What fault does the media have as implied by the author?
3. Identify three countries that may have been affected by intelligence leaks as stated by the viewpoint.

"The media hypocrisy over Trump's intelligence leak," by Marc A. Thiessen, American Enterprise Institute, May 16, 2017. Reprinted by permission.

The media are in a froth over reports that President Trump revealed sensitive intelligence from a liaison partner to the Russian foreign minister and Russian ambassador. *The New York Times* reports:

> *President Trump boasted about highly classified intelligence in a meeting with the Russian foreign minister and ambassador last week, providing details that could expose the source of the information and the manner in which it was collected, a current and a former American government official said Monday. If true, the disclosures, which appear to be inadvertent, are indeed a disaster.*
>
> *The intelligence disclosed by Mr. Trump … was about an Islamic State plot, according to the officials. A Middle Eastern ally that closely guards its own secrets provided the information, which was considered so sensitive that American officials did not share it widely within the United States government or pass it on to other allies….*
>
> *Sharing the information without the express permission of the ally who provided it was a major breach of espionage etiquette, and could jeopardize a crucial intelligence-sharing relationship. In fact, the ally has repeatedly warned American officials that it would cut off access to such sensitive information if it were shared too widely, the former official said. In this case, the fear is that Russia will be able to determine exactly how the information was collected and could disrupt the ally's espionage efforts.*

What the *Times* describes, if true, is indeed a disaster.

But it's hard to take seriously their sudden concern over the "disaster" of exposing sources and methods—including the identity of intelligence partners—from the same news outlets that regularly, and intentionally, published highly classified intelligence in recent years, based on leaks from the Obama administration. The *Times* and other news outlets regularly published "disastrous" stories which damaged US national security and exposed the involvement of US partners.

Consider just a few illustrative examples:

Some argue that the media is complicit in intelligence leaks.

US–Israeli Role in "Stuxnet" Attack on Iran

Where was the outrage when *The New York Times* exposed the US government's cyberattack on Iran's nuclear program, including the fact that Obama personally ordered cyberattacks on the Iranian nuclear program using a computer virus called Stuxnet? The Times cited as sources "members of the President's national security team who were in the [Situation Room]" and even quoted the president asking during a top secret meeting: "Should we shut this thing down?" Only Obama's most trusted national security advisers would have been present when he uttered those words. One of those advisors shared highly classified intelligence with the *Times.*

The Stuxnet leak exposed intelligence sources and methods, including the top secret codename for the program ("Olympic Games") and the involvement of a US ally, Israel. At one point in the *Times* story, a source says the Israelis were responsible for an error in the code which allowed it to replicate itself all around the world. The *Times* directly quotes one of the president's briefers telling him, "We think there was a modification done by the Israelis," adding that, "Mr. Obama, according to officials in the room, asked a series of questions, fearful that the code could do damage outside the plant. The answers came back in hedged terms. Mr. Biden fumed. 'It's got to be the Israelis,' he said. 'They went too far.'"

Where was the concern for the exposure this intelligence or the involvement of our liaison partner? The damage this leak did—both to the operation and the trust between our two countries—is incalculable.

NSA Ability to Access Terrorist Computers Not Connected to the Internet

What about *The New York Times* story in 2014 revealing that the National Security Agency had developed the capability to access computers that are not connected to the Internet?

According to the Times, the NSA uses "a covert channel of radio waves that can be transmitted from tiny circuit boards and USB cards inserted surreptitiously into ... computers" or in some cases "a brief-case-size relay station that intelligence agencies can set up miles away from the target." The Times reported that, "There is no evidence that the NSA has implanted its software or used its radio frequency technology inside the United States." And the NSA confirmed that the "NSA's activities are focused and specifically deployed against—and only against—valid foreign intelligence targets."

So the program posed precisely zero threat to American civil liberties. Publishing it was nothing more than engaging in "espionage porn." But the Times ran it anyway. Where was the concern for national security then?

Identity of the Doctor Who Helped Us Find Bin Laden

Or how about the disclosure of classified operational details of the raid that killed Osama bin Laden, including the identity of the Pakistani doctor who helped us track down bin Laden? ABC News reported that:

> *The Pakistani doctor who aided American intelligence in its mission to kill Osama bin Laden has been convicted of high treason in his home country and sentenced to 33 years in prison plus a fine, Pakistani officials said today.*

Indeed, he is still rotting in a Pakistani prison to this day. Did this exposure by Obama officials bragging about the president's accomplishment have a chilling effect on intelligence cooperation? You bet.

Saudi Double Agent in Yemen

Or how the Obama administration's shameful exposure of the role of a double agent recruited in London by British intelligence in breaking up a new underwear bomb plot in Yemen? *The Guardian* reported at the time:

> *Detailed leaks of operational information about the foiled underwear bomb plot are causing growing anger in the US intelligence community, with former agents blaming the Obama administration for undermining national security and compromising the British services, MI6 and MI5.*
>
> The Guardian *has learned from Saudi sources that the agent was not a Saudi national as was widely reported, but a Yemeni. He was born in Saudi Arabia, in the port city of Jeddah, and then studied and worked in the UK, where he acquired a British passport.*
>
> *Mike Scheur, the former head of the CIA's Bin Laden unit, said the leaking about the nuts and bolts of British involvement was despicable and would make a repeat of the operation difficult.*

Libyan Cooperation in Capture of Al Qaeda Leader

And what about the *Times* story exposing the fact that then-Libyan Prime Minister Ali Zeidan allowed the United States to carry out a special operations raid in Tripoli that captured a senior al-Qaeda leader, Nazih Abdul-Hamed al-Ruqai, known as Abu Anas al-Libi? In a front-page story, "US Officials Say Libya Approved Commando Raids," the *Times* reported that:

> *After months of lobbying by American officials, the Libyans consented 'some time ago'—weeks or perhaps even months—to the United States operations … [according to] more than half a dozen American diplomatic, military, law enforcement, intelligence and other administration*

officials.... The Libyans' consent marks a significant step forward for the Obama administration, which has been criticized by Congressional Republicans for moving too slowly to apprehend the Benghazi suspects.

FAST FACT

Every morning the president receives the President's Daily Brief, a report of classified intelligence.

Not only was a liaison partner's counter-terrorism cooperation exposed, the prime minister was kidnapped in retaliation for approving the raid!

Worse still, the *Times* revealed that a second raid had been planned, but not carried out, "to seize a militia leader suspected of carrying out the Sept. 11, 2012, attacks on the United States diplomatic mission in Benghazi."

Secret US Drone Base in Saudi Arabia

Or how about *The Washington Post* story revealing the existence of a secret US drone base in Saudi Arabia? The Post reported:

> *President Obama's plan to install his counterterrorism adviser as director of the CIA has opened the administration to new scrutiny over the targeted-killing policies it has fought to keep hidden from the public, as well as the existence of a previously secret drone base in Saudi Arabia.... The Obama administration's targeted-killing program has relied on a growing constellation of drone bases operated by the CIA and the US military's Joint Special Operations Command. The only strike intentionally targeting a US citizen, a 2011 attack that killed al-Qaeda operative Anwar al-Awlaki, was carried out in part by CIA drones flown from a secret base in Saudi Arabia.*

Did this expose and endanger the cooperation of a critical US intelligence partner?

Special Operations Activities Against Al-Qaeda in Africa

On June 13, 2012, the *Washington Post* reported: "The US military is expanding its secret intelligence operations across Africa, establishing a network of small air bases to spy on terrorist hideouts from the fringes of the Sahara to jungle terrain along the equator, according to documents and people involved in the project." The article exposed that, "Under a classified surveillance program code-named Creek Sand, dozens of US personnel and contractors have come to [Burkina Faso] in recent years to establish a small air base on the military side of the international airport." The Burkina Faso foreign minister, caught by surprise by the leak, is quoted as pleading, "This cooperation should be very, very discreet. We should not show to al-Qaeda that we are now working with the Americans."

Too late.

These are just a few examples. The list of leaks and liaison partners exposed during the Obama years goes on and on.

None of this excuses Trump's accidentally sharing top-secret intelligence with Russian officials. But it takes chutzpah for the media to express outrage over his apparently inadvertent disclosure of classified information—or to feign concern over the effect his actions might have on cooperation by our intelligence partners in the fight against terror—when they regularly published often intentional leaks from Obama administration that exposed sources and methods and endangered our national security.

Trump may have stumbled badly in his meeting with the Russians, but he has a long way to go before he does the kind of damage that President Obama and his team of intelligence sieves did—with the help of *The New York Times* and other news outlets now crowing over his error.

EVALUATING THE AUTHOR'S ARGUMENTS:

In this viewpoint, Marc A. Thiessen brings to mind an old saying, that those who live in glass houses should not throw stones. Explain this using two or more examples from Thiessen's viewpoint.

Viewpoint 3

Investigation and Prosecution of Guilty Individuals Should Continue

"During the last several years, we have received roughly 50 crime reports each year of leaks to the media of classified information."

Steven Aftergood

In the following viewpoint, Steven Aftergood analyzes the process that occurs when federal crimes, including the unauthorized disclosure of classified information, are committed. Aftergood provides insight into a rather complicated procedure of crime reporting, and the later investigation into said crimes. Aftergood shares historical information about media disclosure and recent attempts by Congress to tighten laws about disclosure. Steven Aftergood directs the FAS Project on Government Secrecy at the Federation of American Scientists. The Project works to reduce the scope of national security secrecy and to promote public access to government information.

"'Crimes Reports' and the Leak Referral Process," by Steven Aftergood, Federation of American Scientist, December 17, 2012. https://fas.org/blogs/secrecy/2012/12/crimes_reports. Reprinted by Permission.

AS YOU READ, CONSIDER THE FOLLOWING QUESTIONS:

1. What are "crimes reports" according to the author?
2. Which agency investigates leaks of classified information according to Aftergood?
3. What happened in the 1990s that is significant as stated in the viewpoint?

"Crimes reports" are official notifications that are sent by U.S. intelligence agencies to the Department of Justice when an unauthorized disclosure of classified information (or another potential federal crime) is believed to have occurred. Crimes reporting is required by statute, by executive order, and by interagency agreement between the Attorney General and the heads of intelligence agencies.

"We file crimes reports every week," said George J. Tenet in a discussion of leaks during his 1997 confirmation hearing to be Director of Central Intelligence.

"Say again?" said Sen. Robert Kerrey, who may have been unfamiliar with the term used by Mr. Tenet.

"We file crimes reports with the Attorney General every week about leaks, and we're never successful in litigating one," Mr. Tenet said.

In general, information or allegations concerning criminal activity by government employees should be reported to the Attorney General pursuant to 28 U.S.C. 535, "Investigation of crimes involving Government officers and employees."

More particularly, Executive Order 12333 (section 1.6) on United States Intelligence Activities requires the heads of intelligence agencies to "report to the Attorney General possible violations of Federal criminal laws by employees and of specified Federal criminal laws by any other person as provided in procedures agreed upon by the Attorney General and the head of the department, agency, or establishment concerned…."

The unusual term "crimes reports" derives from those procedures, which are set forth in a 1995 Memorandum of Understanding (MOU): Reporting of Information Concerning Federal Crimes,

The Department of Justice receives crime reports whenever US intelligence agencies believe an unauthorized disclosure has occurred.

signed by Attorney General Janet Reno and the heads of six other agencies.

Though it is rarely cited in public discussions of leak policy, this MOU provides the structural framework for intelligence community reporting to the Justice Department regarding leaks of classified information, among other potential crimes.

"This Agreement requires each employee of the Agency to report to the General Counsel or IG facts or circumstances that reasonably indicate to the employee than an employee of an intelligence agency has committed, is committing, or will commit a violation of federal criminal law." Then, "If a preliminary inquiry reveals that there is a reasonable belief for the allegations, the General Counsel will follow the reporting requirements" for submission of "crimes reports."

Intelligence agency employees are also required to report to the General Counsel of their agency information about certain violations of criminal law that are committed by persons who are not employees of an intelligence agency– specifically including "unauthorized disclosure of classified information."

Fast Fact

By the summer of 2017, the Justice Department had almost tripled the number of cases it investigated concerning disclosure of classified information.

Crimes reports in such cases are to be submitted to the Department of Justice, which "shall maintain a record of all special crimes reports received from the Agency." If, in addition, the agency determines that no public disclosure of classified information would result from further investigation or prosecution of the matter, then it is also to be reported to the appropriate federal investigative agency.

"During the last several years, we have received roughly 50 crime reports each year of leaks to the media of classified information," said Attorney General Janet Reno in June 2000 testimony before a closed hearing of the Senate Intelligence Committee. (Although she said "crime report", the preferred locution seems to be "crimes report.")

"Because of the large number of leaks and the recognition that the Department and the FBI have limited investigative resources, intelligence agencies do not request criminal investigations of every unauthorized disclosure of classified information," she said. "Instead, they request investigations of the most damaging leaks, usually around 20-25 cases a year for the last several years. We have opened investigations into almost all of the leaks requested by the victim agencies."

However, AG Reno explained, "before opening a criminal investigation, the Criminal Division generally requires the agency requesting the investigation to submit the answers to eleven specific questions regarding what was leaked and who had access to it.... We believe that the eleven questions are essentially the equivalent of filing a police report. They provide the information we need to determine whether a criminal investigation is likely to be productive and, if so, where to start."

A copy of the DoJ Media Leak Questionnaire with the eleven questions is available here: https://fas.org/irp/agency/doj/leak-questions.pdf.

The figure of 50 crimes reports per year noted by the Attorney General in 2000 is consistent with George Tenet's 1997 statement that crimes reports on leaks were being filed "every week."

But a CIA Inspector General report in 2000 (on the handling of classified information by CIA director John Deutch) said that "Records of the [CIA] Office of General Counsel indicate there were an average of 200 written crimes reports submitted to DoJ each year for the period 1995–1998."

If that is correct, then presumably the larger figure includes reports of federal crimes other than unauthorized disclosures.

Between September 2001 and February 2008, the Federal Bureau of Investigation initiated and closed the investigation of 85 reported leaks of classified intelligence information, "all of which concerned unauthorized disclosures of classified information to the media," FBI Director Robert S. Mueller III told the Senate Intelligence Committee in 2008. "None of these cases reached prosecution," he said. But as of February 2008, "21 such cases are [still] under investigation." ("Classified Intelligence Leaks, 2001-2008," *Secrecy News*, July 15, 2009).

Between 2005 and 2009, U.S. intelligence agencies submitted 183 "referrals" to the Department of Justice reporting unauthorized disclosures of classified intelligence. Based on those referrals or on its own initiative, the FBI opened 26 leak investigations, and the investigations led to the identification of 14 suspects. ("FBI Found 14 Leak Suspects in Past Five Years," *Secrecy News*, June 21, 2010).

Though it is hard to be certain, the most sustained and prolific leaking of Top Secret and compartmented information may have occurred during the late 1990s when such leaks appeared every few days in the reporting of *Washington Times* reporter Bill Gertz.

"It's getting a little tiring to see this constant source of leaks to the *Washington Times* of classified intelligence documents," State Department spokesman Nicholas Burns told the *Weekly Standard* in an otherwise admiring profile of Mr. Gertz in 1996. ("He Drives Them Crazy" by Matthew Rees, December 1, 1996.)

No arrests or prosecutions resulted from that "constant source of leaks," though it eventually diminished.

Meanwhile, the current Congress is still considering new constraints on disclosure of classified information that go well beyond anything the executive branch has requested or considers prudent.

Robert Litt, the general counsel of the Office of the Director of National Intelligence, recently expressed some criticism of the congressional anti-leak initiative.

"We have discussed with the Intelligence Committee our concern that some of the proposals in their legislation really would not have any deterrent impact or punitive impact on leaks, and might in fact have an adverse impact on the free flow of information to the American people," Mr. Litt told an American Bar Association meeting last month.

But it is not clear whether the Senate Intelligence Committee, which has not held an open hearing in almost a year, would be moved by appeals to "the free flow of information to the American people."

EVALUATING THE AUTHOR'S ARGUMENTS:

In this viewpoint, Steven Aftergood gives insight into the process of investigation that occurs surrounding leaks of classified information. Briefly outline this procedure and comment on it using the information you've learned from previous viewpoints.

Viewpoint 4

Leaking Does Not Deserve the Same Punishment As Espionage

Duncan Campbell

"The British government has received recommendations for a "future-proofed" new Espionage Act that would put leaking and whistleblowing in the same category as spying for foreign powers."

In the following viewpoint, Duncan Campbell analyzes upcoming changes in legislation by the United Kingdom concerning leaking of classified information and whistleblowing activities. Duncan maintains that the proposed changes in British law will be far reaching when it comes to individuals charged with disclosure of information. Offering many examples, Campbell argues that new laws will certainly not be good for the public as public knowledge gained from whistleblowing is vital to society. Duncan Campbell is an investigative journalist specializing in issues of surveillance, privacy, and civil liberties.

"Planned Espionage Act could jail journos and whistleblowers as spies," by Duncan Campbell, The Register (theregister.co.uk), February 10, 2017. Reprinted by permission.

AS YOU READ, CONSIDER THE FOLLOWING QUESTIONS:

1. According to Campbell, who might be prosecuted because of these new laws?
2. As reported in the viewpoint, do the new laws effect the United States?
3. How has espionage changed in the digital era as stated by the author?

The proposed law update is an attempt to ban reporting of future big data leaks.

The British government has received recommendations for a "future-proofed" new Espionage Act that would put leaking and whistleblowing in the same category as spying for foreign powers.

That threatens leakers and journalists with the same extended jail sentences as foreign agents. Sentences would apply even if—like Edward Snowden or Chelsea Manning—the leaker was not British, or in Britain, or was intent on acting in the public interest.

The proposals have been slammed by journalists who faced down British and US government threats after publishing Edward Snowden's sensational revelations in 2013.

The UK Law Commission's recommendations are contained in a 326-page consultation paper titled Protection of Official Data.

"It is alarming that such a far-reaching proposed reform of laws which could be used to jail whistleblowers and journalists should have been drafted without any adequate consultation with free speech organisations," Alan Rusbridger, the former *Guardian* editor who published the Snowden revelations, told *The Reg*.

According to the commission, the proposed "redrafted offence" of espionage would "be capable of being committed by someone who not only communicates information, but also by someone who obtains or gathers it."

There should, it says, be "no restriction on who can commit the offence," including hackers, leakers, elected politicians, journalists, and NGOs.

With laws like those proposed in England, journalists who report classified information could be punished as severely as double agents.

If the proposed law had been in force in 2013, the Cabinet Office could have thrown Rusbridger in prison simply for handling copies of documents Edward Snowden passed to his reporters.

As it was, Rusbridger was threatened with a gagging order and jail, and forced secretly to destroy newspaper computers when the government tried to block the Snowden revelations from being published.

Although a US citizen and intelligence agency contractor, Snowden had wide access to secret reports and plans from Britain's electronic spying agency GCHQ through a top-secret, Wikipedia-style system called GCWiki.

Snowden copied tens of thousands of GCHQ documents from this system and gave them to *The Guardian* journalists who visited him in Hong Kong in 2013.

The Dangers of 'Public Interest'

David Leigh, The Guardian's former investigations editor who helped handle the prize-winning Snowden and Wikileaks investigations,

Fast Fact

In the United Kingdom, intelligence gathering is governed by three sets of laws: the Intelligence Services Act, the Human Rights Act, and the Regulation of Investigatory Powers Act.

described the Law Commission's proposed changes as "a giant leap backwards to the bad old days when public-interest journalists went in fear."

Jim Killock, chief executive of the Open Rights Group (ORG), told *The Reg*: "Public-interest whistleblowing is vital to society. Without it no one could have known the secret scale of global surveillance."

In a new extension to the proposed secrecy law, official economic information could also be covered by the same heavy penalties. The Law Commission report asks, rhetorically, if "sensitive information relating to the economy [should] be brought within the scope of the legislation... in so far as it relates to national security."

Furthermore, British Embassies abroad, intelligence and security offices, and data centres not officially publicised by the government would be designated as "prohibited places" or "protected sites," making it an offence to publish information about them or to "approach, inspect, pass over or enter" for any "purpose prejudicial" to national security.

The report nowhere defines "national security". The commission claims that this is acceptable under current international human rights law. The proposed law would replace four Official Secrets Acts dating back to 1911, as well as a raft of other government restrictions on releasing information, providing extra powers instead. There should be no statutory public-interest defence for anyone accused of offences, the Commission say.

As if this isn't bad enough, the commission has admitted to The Register that its proposals were devised without meaningful input from rights groups or journalists. In doing so, the commission undermined its own claim to have consulted widely in preparing their proposals.

Consulting 'Too Much Work'

Law Commissioner Professor David Ormerod QC claimed in a recent "exclusive" Daily Telegraph report: "We've scrutinised the law and consulted widely with… media and human rights organisations."

The report listed 21 government departments and police, intelligence and security agencies that were consulted, alongside 18 judges, lawyers and others—and three NGOs.

ORG was one of the three NGOs listed in the report as having being "consulted widely." However, ORG's Killock told *The Register*: "There was no consultation. There were some emails with our legal adviser about having a meeting, which petered out without any discussion or detail being given."

ORG's adviser was then told in April 2016 by Law Commission lawyer and Oxford University lecturer Karl Laird: "Over the summer we will be holding an open consultation asking for views on our consultation paper, so there will be that opportunity." But there was no consultation or further communication, according to ORG. The commission say that the job they were given proved too big to have time to talk to journalists and editors.

Killock described the commission's first fact-finding phase as: "Shoddy—they should have established the facts for their initial review by a wide inquiry, not by taking a lead from government security advocates."

National Union of Journalists communications officer Sarah Kavanagh said they were told nothing and were never consulted about the Law Commission review. "The first we heard was reading a [press report]," she said.

The Guardian told *The Reg* that it had been contacted last year, and then attended a short meeting at legal offices in May 2016 together with a *Times* adviser.

It was "high-level very general chat" without specific proposals. Laird promised the media lawyers that he would "keep [them] updated." There was then no further communication or discussion.

The Law Commission confirmed to *The Register* this week that most British NGOs concerned with human rights and free expression were not consulted about the review, including the Bureau of Investigative Journalism, the Centre for Investigative Reporting,

Reporters Without Borders, Amnesty International, Article 19, Open Democracy, Privacy International, Index On Censorship and the writers group PEN.

A Law Commission spokesman told *The Reg*: "We had planned to consult in the summer, but... it became a larger piece of work than we anticipated.

"We undertook a pre-consultation fact-finding mission which informed and shaped our consultation questions and provisional conclusions. We... engaged with what we considered a wide range of stakeholders in an initial fact-finding mission who we felt could shape our initial thoughts."

He added that the report was not press released and was deliberately only initially provided solely to The Telegraph because "it's a nuanced issue. We wanted to secure an opinion editorial first."

The Ball Is in Your Court

The commission says its final recommendations will be "shaped by the views of those who respond to our open consultation, which is now open until April 3." They then expect to publish a revised report, which could include a first draft of an Espionage Act.

The changes to the law have been proposed following examination by the commission at the request of the Cabinet Office. Number 10 had asked officials to examine "the law surrounding breaches of protected government data" soon after the 2015 General Election and two years after *The Guardian* had published the revelations from Edward Snowden, transforming global understanding about the vast scale of secret electronic surveillance.

The Cabinet Office asked for "an effective and coherent legal response to unauthorised disclosures." The review was also intended to "examine provisions that criminalise those who illegitimately obtain or attempt to obtain official information."

The inquiry's terms of reference refer directly to large-scale data leaks, asking the commission to review "the effect of technological change on the way in which data is stored, shared and understood, and [to] determine whether the current law needs to be reformed properly to account for these changes."

The Law Commission agreed to "research potential improvements to these sanctions."

Because 21st century leaks are almost invariably digital, the commission claims: "The volume of information that can be disclosed without authorisation is much greater... this means that the ability to cause damage to the national interest has also increased.

"Before the digital era, anyone engaging in espionage would be limited as to how much information they could access. But now online communications and storage means the volume of information and associated risk is of a very different scale."

The sentences available should rise from 2 to 14 years imprisonment, the commission suggests.

Rusbridger told *The Reg*: "The consultation paper is very one-sided. The Law Commission must urgently consult more widely—and act more independently."

The Cabinet Office refused to say whether a draft Bill would be requested or legislation intended. "As the work is ongoing and no final conclusions have been made, it would be inappropriate to comment."

EVALUATING THE AUTHOR'S ARGUMENTS:

In this viewpoint, Duncan Campbell analyzes how changes in British law would affect persons attempting to leak classified materials. Should the US adopt tougher measures such as this? Why or why not?

Viewpoint 5

Whistleblowers Must Be Protected

Eric Connon

"Many government employees or contractors do not have the legal and institutional protections needed to come forward safely."

In the following viewpoint, Eric Connon argues that whistleblowers, people that for a variety of reasons feel it is necessary to leak classified documents, should be protected. Connon presents the example of a US government contractor, Edward Snowden, who released a trove of documents to journalists. Connon suggests implementations to protect whistleblowers at the domestic and international level since they are acting in the interests of the public's right to know and holding governments accountable. Eric Connon is a Judicial Law Clerk and graduate from Case Western Reserve University Law School.

AS YOU READ, CONSIDER THE FOLLOWING QUESTIONS:

1. According to Connon, who is Edward Snowden?
2. Why did Snowden flee the US, according to the viewpoint?
3. As stated by the author, what are two protections that whistleblowers should be afforded?

"Are Intelligence-Community Leakers Internationally Protected Whistleblowers or Simply "Whistling in the Dark"? Assessing the Protections Afforded to Intelligence-Community Whistle blowers under International Law," by Eric Connon, 67 Case W. Res. L. Rev. 897 (2017) Available at: http://scholarlycommons.law.case.edu/caselrev/vol67/iss3/14

Americans are divided regarding how they feel about Edward Snowden's actions.

In June 2013, *The Guardian* published a series of groundbreaking articles revealing the unfettered access of the U.S. government to internet and phone records, either directly or through FISA[1] court-ordered acquisition of records held by private corporations.[2] The source of these revelations was an unknown government contractor, Edward Snowden, who supplied this information to journalists from a hotel room in Hong Kong. As evidence, Snowden had four laptops in his possession containing, by one estimation, more than 1.5 million classified documents[3] he accessed while employed by the National Security Agency ("NSA") in Hawaii.[4] The release of Snowden's identity was not a mistake or the result of an investigation, but rather the intentional act of a man who considered himself to be, as conveyed by his journalist-contact Glenn Greenwald, a whistleblower.[5] Snowden asserted, "I have no intention of hiding who I am because I know I have done nothing wrong."[6] The Obama Administration, however, did not consider Snowden's public disclosures to constitute legitimate whistle-blowing.[7] On June 14, 2013, the U.S. government issued a complaint against Snowden[8] for theft

Fast Fact

As of January 2017, it is expected that Edward Snowden will remain in Russia until 2020.

of government property[9] and espionage.[10] Congress also sent an official request to Hong Kong for his extradition.[11] Rather than return to the United States and face criminal sanction, Snowden instead cast about the international community for a safe haven.[12]

Though Snowden's subsequent transnational trek consisted only of a trip from Hong Kong to Moscow, it was accompanied by uncertainty, widespread media speculation, and heightened diplomatic stakes.[13] Snowden checked out of his Hong Kong hotel room on June 14th and disappeared until June 23rd, when he boarded a flight to Moscow.[14]

Snowden faced substantial hurdles in his efforts to resist extradition and secure safe passage to a country willing to grant asylum. He had intended for Moscow to be a temporary layover to allow for a connecting flight to Cuba, but the U.S. government derailed that plan by cancelling Snowden's passport, preventing further international travel.[15] He found himself stranded in Sheremetyevo Airport, applying for asylum status in more than twenty countries, including China, Austria, Finland, India, Spain, and Switzerland.[16] Bolivia, Ecuador, Nicaragua, and Venezuela offered him permanent asylum, but Snowden chose to apply for temporary asylum in Russia because of concerns that he could not access a safe, direct route to one of those four countries from Moscow.[17] Russia declined to extradite Snowden to the United States and, instead, granted him a one-year temporary asylum,[18] which Russia extended for three more years in the summer of 2014.[19]

Edward Snowden's case illustrates the challenging predicament for intelligence-community employees[20] who leak information exposing perceived government misconduct. Though many government employees or contractors may wish to challenge what they perceive as unethical, illegal, or corrupt practices within the workplace, many do not have the legal and institutional protections needed to come forward safely.[21] Depending on the nature of the information disclosed, attempts to bring complaints and revelations to the press can result in criminal charges.[22] Snowden's case is noteworthy because, unlike other intelligence-community leakers,[23] he evaded domestic law enforcement and entered the international legal realm.

Snowden's travails reveal much about the current protections afforded to intelligence-community leakers under domestic and inter- national law. Should Edward Snowden and other leakers be classified as whistleblowers, deserving of protection under domestic whistleblower laws? If not, do they instead qualify for the extraterritorial protections afforded to refugees or asylees under international law? If the leakers do constitute whistleblowers, but are denied safe harbor under both domestic and international law, what can or should be done to better address and protect those employees and contractors exposing government misconduct?

[…]

The Value of Whistleblowers in the Intelligence Community

The international community should strive to improve whistleblower protections for intelligence-community employees at both the domestic and international level. The need for secure internal reporting channels and clear guidelines on appropriate timing and methods for disclosing to the media is apparent from the heated discussion on the legacy of Edward Snowden. Because Snowden found whistleblower protections for U.S. intelligience-community employees to be insufficient, he took steps to seize and disclose classified documents publicly, with- out the benefit of knowing what or how much to disclose. Improving the domestic and international legal protections afforded to whistle- blowers will serve the public interest while limiting mass leaks of classified state secrets.

Even Edward Snowden's detractors concede that his disclosures provided some public benefit.[203] Snowden's leaks "launch[ed] an ongoing national debate about the NSA's proper role in private affairs [and] [c]oncern about these activities was so great that President Obama appointed a panel of advisors to study NSA surveillance, which ultimately recommended strictly curtailing the NSA's ability to engage in warrantless data collection."[204] Many credit Snowden with heightened public awareness of digital privacy issues[205] and increased judicial scrutiny of government intelligence-gathering tactics.[206] Most commentators will concede that there was a benefit to the public that came from Snowden's disclsoures.

There are lingering questions, however, as to the potential cost. Many allege that Snowden released far too much information that exposed lawful, essential government programs.[207] The House Intelligence Committee alleges that "[s]ome of Snowden's disclosures exacerbated and accelarated existing trends that diminished the [intelligence community's] capabilities to collect against legitimate foreign intelligence targets, while others resulted in the loss of intelligence streams that had saved American lives."[208] While defenders contend that any damage done by Snowden's disclosures is overblown[209] or greatly outweighed by the benefit,[210] his critics charge that his acts have benefited terrorist organizations[211] and cost lives and money.[212]

Improvements to domestic and international whistleblower protection may allow societies to benefit from good-faith disclosures while avoiding the drawbacks cited by Snowden detractors. States should implement effective internal reporting channels and allow whistleblowers direct access to independent oversight bodies. Public disclosures should also be permitted to whistleblowers in the event an internal reporting channel fails, but with clearly communicated limitations on when such disclosure is appropriate and how much material may be released to the public. Upgraded reporting mechanisms and greater protections for intelligence-community whistleblowers would alert the government to potential abuses and waste while preventing the possible damage to national security interests that may accompany mass leaks of classified material. If states are unwilling to provide secure reporting procedures for intelligence-community whistleblowers, the international community should adjust the refugee and asylum legal frameworks to provide that missing protection to those that report government abuses and overreach under the threat of unwarranted retaliation.

Endnotes

1. The Foreign Intelligence Service Court ("FISA") was established under the Foreign Intelligence Service Act in 1978. See generally United States Foreign Surveillance Court, http://www.fisc.uscourts.gov/ [https:// perma.cc/F7KB-CSY9] (last visited Oct. 18, 2016) ("The Foreign Intelligence Surveillance Court was established by Con-

gress in 1978. The Court entertains applications made by the United States Government for approval of electronic surveillance, physical search, and certain other forms of inves- tigative actions for foreign intelligence purposes.").

2. See generally Glenn Greenwald, NSA Collecting Phone Records of Millions of Verizon Customers Daily, The Guardian (June 6, 2013, 6:05 AM), https://www.theguardian.com/world/2013/jun/06/nsa-phone-records- verizon-court-order [https://perma.cc/NQC7-FBKY]; Barton Gellman & Laura Poitras, U.S., British Intelligence Mining Data from Nine U.S. Internet Companies in Broad Secret Program, Wash. Post (June 7, 2013), https://www.washingtonpost.com/investigations/us-intelligence-mining-data-from-nine-us-internet-companies-in-broad-secret- program/2013/06/06/3a0c0da8-cebf-11e2-8845-d970ccb04497_story.html[https://perma.cc/5X8T-WMCL]; Glenn Greenwald & Ewen MacAskill, Boundless Informant: The NSA's Secret Tool to Track Global Surveillance Data, The Guardian (June 11, 2013, 9:00 AM), http://www.theguardian.com/world/2013/jun/08/nsa-boundless-informant- global-datamining [https://perma.cc/JR49-M49R].
3. H.R. Permanent Select Comm. on Intelligence, Executive Sum- mary of Review of the Unauthorized Disclosures of Former National Security Agency Contractor Edward Snowden (2016) [hereinafter Intelligence Committee Executive Summary]. This number cited by the Intelligence Committee has been criticized in some quarters. See, e.g., Barton Gellman, The House Intelligence Committee's Terrible, Horrible, Very Bad Snowden Report, The Century Found. (Sept. 16, 2016), https://tcf.org/content/commentary/house-intelligence-committees- terrible-horrible-bad-snowden-report/ [https://perma.cc/8P53-L4KS] ("In fact, the nation's most senior intelligence officers, no admirers of Snowden, have repeatedly said they can only surmise the number."); Trevor Timm, The Washington Post is Wrong: Edward Snowden Should be Pardoned, The Guardian (Sept. 19, 2016, 4:28 PM), https://www.theguardian.com/ commentisfree/2016/sep/19/washington-post-wrong-edward-snowden-pardon [https://perma.cc/DM84-CW7E] ("Even the former NSA director himself admitted that the 1.5m number only represented the documents that Snowden 'touched', and officials didn't know how many he actually took.").
4. Glenn Greenwald, Ewen MacAskill & Laura Poitras, Edward Snowden: The Whistleblower Behind the NSA Surveillance Revelations, The Guardian (June 11, 2013, 9:00 AM), https://www.theguardian.com/world/2013/jun/ 09/edward-snowden-nsa-whistleblower-surveillance [https://perma.cc/TQN8- RENK].
5. Id.
6. Id.
7. See Aamer Madhani & David Jackson, Obama: I Don't See Snowden as a Patriot, USA Today (Aug. 9, 2013, 9:20 PM), http://www.usatoday.com/ story/news/politics/2013/08/09/obama-news-conference/2636191/ [https:// perma.cc/C2YA-HFL6].
8. Criminal Complaint, United States v. Snowden, No. 1:13 CR 265, (E.D. Va. June 14, 2013).
9. 18 U.S.C. 641 (2012) ("Whoever . . . steals . . . or knowingly converts to his use or the use of another, or without authority, sells, conveys or disposes of any record . . . of the United States or of any department or agency thereof . . . [s]hall be fined under this title or imprisoned not more than ten years, or both . . . .").
10. 18 U.S.C. 793(d) (2012); 18 U.S.C. 798(a)(3) (2012); see also Criminal Complaint, supra note 8.

11. Mirren Gidda, Edward Snowden and the NSA Files—Timeline, The Guardian (Aug. 21, 2013, 5:54 PM), http://www.theguardian.com/world/ 2013/jun/23/edward-snowden-nsa-files-timeline [https://perma.cc/GP2M- ZXE3].

12. Haroon Siddique, Edward Snowden Asylum: Countries Approached and Their Responses, The Guardian (July 4, 2013, 11:38 AM), http:// www.theguardian.com/world/2013/jul/02/edward-snowden-nsa-asylum- application-list-countries [https://perma.cc/DHJ3-V2T4] (citing Snowden's statement that he had applied for asylum in a total of 21 countries to that date).

13. See, e.g., Michael Pearson, Matt Smith & Jethro Mullen, Snowden's Asylum Options Dwindle, CNN (July 2, 2013, 7:15 PM), http://www.cnn .com/2013/07/02/politics/nsa-leak/ [https://perma.cc/QX49-BNWV] (describing Snowden's limited options).

14. Id.

15. Id.

16. Siddique, supra note 12 (including European countries such as Iceland, Italy, Ireland, Norway, and Poland).

17. Phil Black, Laura Smith-Spark & Michael Martinez, Snowden Meets with Rights Groups, Seeks Temporary Asylum in Russia, CNN (July 13, 2013, 9:29 AM), http://www.cnn.com/2013/07/12/world/europe/russia-us- snowden/ [https://perma.cc/K6H2-RBDS]; see also Emily C. Kendall, Note, Sanctuary in the 21st Century: The Unique Asylum Exception to the Extradition Rule, 23 Mich. St. Int'l L. Rev. 153, 170 (2014) ("Four countries offered him permanent asylum: Bolivia, Ecuador, Nicaragua, and Venezuela. However, Mr. Snowden chose to apply for temporary asylum in Russia because he did not feel he would be able to safely travel to any Latin American country, since Bolivian President Evo Morales's flight from Russia to Bolivia had been rerouted and denied airspace in France, Spain, and Italy due to suspicions that Mr. Snowden was on board." (emphasis in original) (citations omitted)).

18. Steven Lee Myers & Andrew E. Kramer, Defiant Russia Grants Snowden Year's Asylum, N.Y. Times (Aug. 1, 2013), http://www.nytimes.com/ 2013/08/02/world/europe/edward-snowden-russia.html? [https://perma.cc/ 23XB-FBFT].

19. Isabel Gorst, Russia Gives Edward Snowden Asylum for Three More Years, L.A. Times (Aug. 7, 2014, 10:37 AM), http://www.latimes.com/world/ europe/la-fg-russia-snowden-asylum-20140807-story.html [https://perma.cc/ J5W8-3UYD].

20. The focus of this Note is on the employees of agencies and governmental departments (including employees of contractors for those bodies) whose "principal function [is] conducting foreign intelligence or counterintelligence activities," including, but not limited to, the Central Intelligence Agency, Defense Intelligence Agency, National Imagery and Mapping Agency, National Reconnaissance Office, National Security Agency, and Federal Bureau of Investigation. See Rodney M. Perry, Cong. Research Serv., R43765, Intelligence Whistleblower Protections: In Brief 2 (2014) (citations omitted) (describing the agencies covered by intelligence agency whistleblower statutes).

21. Simon Wolfe, Mark Worth, Suelette Dreyfus & A J Brown, Whistleblower Protection Rules in G20 Countries: The Next Action Plan, Blueprint for Free Speech 1, 21 (2014), https://www.griffith.edu.au/__data/ assets/pdf_file/0010/619075/Whistleblower-Protection-Rules-in-G20- Countries-The-Next__-Action-Plan-June-2014.pdf [https://perma.cc/P5DZ- TVG4] (indicating that only two G20 countries have "very/quite compre- hensive provisions outlining what procedures public sector organizations must put in place").

22. Id. at 59 (noting the U.S. government's prosecution of intelligence- community leakers such as Thomas Drake, John Kiriakou, Bradley Manning, and Edward Snowden).
23. This Note uses the word "leaker" with regard to the high profile intelligence- community figures discussed within, including Edward Snowden. There is considerable debate as to whether those figures constitute legitimate whistle- blowers and the standard use of the term "whistleblower" presupposes their legal status. See Dana Farrington, What is Meant by the Term 'Whistle- Blower,' NPR (June 10, 2013, 1:38 PM), http://www.npr.org/sections/ thetwo-way/2013/06/10/190380255/what-we-mean-when-we-say- whistleblower [https://perma.cc/G9LQ-GGPW] (discussing the use of the term whistleblower with regard to Edward Snowden and NPR's decision to instead use the term "leaker" in its reporting).
203. See, e.g., Kaplan, supra note 97 (recognizing that "some of [Snowden's] leaks did have social and political benefits"); Editorial, supra note 97 (noting that "[i]t's fair to say we owe these necessary reforms [of NSA programs] to Mr. Snowden").
204. Kwoka, supra note 59, at 1407 (citations omitted).
205. See, e.g., Lee Rainie & Mary Madden, Americans' Privacy Strategies Post-Snowden, Pew Research Ctr. (Mar. 16, 2015), http://www. pewinternet.org/2015/03/16/americans-privacy-strategies-post-snowden/ [https://perma.cc/XD6M-5JWY] (finding that 30% of all adults "have taken at least one step to hide or shield their information from the government" and 22% of all adults say "they have changed the patterns of their own use of various technological platforms 'a great deal' or 'somewhat' since the Snowden revelations").
206. See Trevor Timm, The Snowden Effect: New Privacy Wins Await After Data Transfer Ruling, The Guardian (Oct. 8 2015), https://www. theguardian.com/comment-isfree/2015/oct/08/snowden-effect-new-privacy- wins-data-transfer-ruling [https://perma.cc/GR5R-37NU] ("[O]ur digital rights is [sic] unquestionably more protected than it was when the leaks started. And with the coming court cases over the next year or two, the seismic shift will undoubtedly continue to occur.").
207. See, e.g., David Remnick, Going the Distance: On and Off the Road with Barack Obama, The New Yorker (Jan. 27, 2014), http://www.newyorker. com/magazine/2014/01/27/going-the-distance-david-remnick [https:// perma.cc/HJF4-EF57] (reporting that President Obama described Snowden as a "twenty-nine-year-old [who ended up having] free rein to basically dump a mountain of information, much of which is definitely legal, definitely necessary for national security, and [is] properly . . . classified[.]").
208. Intelligence Committee Executive Summary, supra note 3, at 1.
209. See, e.g., Eric Schmitt & Michael S. Schmidt, Qaeda Plot Leak Has Undermined U.S. Intelligence, N.Y. Times (Sept. 29, 2013), http:// www.nytimes.com/2013/09/30/us/qaeda-plot-leak-has-undermined-us- intelligence.html [https://perma.cc/TQ9L-27GF] ("[S]ome government analysts and senior officials have made a startling finding: the impact of a leaked terrorist plot by Al Qaeda in August has caused more immediate damage to American counterterrorism efforts than the thousands of classified documents disclosed by Edward Snowden . . . .").
210. Gellman, supra note 3 ("I believe Snowden's disclosures did a lot more good than harm, but I do not share the view of some of his fans that he did no damage at all.").
211. See e.g., Michael Hirsh, 'It's All Back in Snowden's Lap,' Politico (Nov. 17, 2015), http://www.politico.com/magazine/story/2015/11/paris-attack- isis-snowden-michael-

morell-interview-cia-213373 [https://perma.cc/GBL6- 4AAM] (quoting Michael Morrell, former acting head of the CIA, as saying "[f]irst, ISIS went to school on how we were collecting intelligence on terrorist organizations by using telecommunications technologies. And when they learned that from the Snowden disclosures, they were able to adapt to it and essentially go silent."); Aaron Cooper, NSA: Snowden Leaks Hurt Ability to Track Terrorists, CNN (Feb. 23, 2015), http:// www.cnn.com/2015/02/23/politics/nsa-surveillance-north-korea/ [https:// perma.cc/KZ27-CFE3] (quoting the head of the National Security Agency who claimed that the Snowden revelations "had a material impact in our ability to generate insights as to what counterterrorism, what terrorist groups around the world are doing . . . ."). But see Natasha Bertrand, Cyber Expert: Idea that Snowden Leaks Facilitated Paris Attacks is 'A Fantastic Work of Intellectual Fiction,' Bus. Insider (Nov. 20, 2015), http://www.businessinsider.com/edwardsnowdenparisattacks201511 [https:// perma.cc/E3X4-GR95] (quoting CEO of cybersecurity firm stating that "[t]here is no evidence at all that the Snowden leaks contributed or altered the kind of terrorist activity that ISIS and Al Qaeda do . . . .").

212. Intelligence Committee Executive Summary, supra note 3, at 2 ("[E]ven by a conservative estimate, the U.S. Government has spent hundreds of millions of dollars, and will eventually spend billions, to attempt to mitigate the damage Snowden caused.").

EVALUATING THE AUTHOR'S ARGUMENTS:

In this viewpoint, Eric Connon argues that whistleblowers play a vital role in society. He contends that the international community should improve protections for these individuals. Do you agree or disagree? Support your opinion with facts from the viewpoint.

Facts About Classified Intelligence and Leaks

Editor's note: These facts can be used in reports to add credibility when making important points or claims.

Levels of Classification

- Top Secret—Highest level of classification, information if released would cause exceptionally grave damage to the national security.
- Secret—Second highest level of classification, information if released would cause serious damage to the national security.
- Confidential—Information at this level is the least restricted and deemed to cause the least amount of damage to the national security if released.
- Restricted—This level of classification is no longer in use, and was discontinued in 1953.
- Codewords have also been used to further sensitize classified materials. The words *umbra*, *talent-keyhole*, *ruff*, or *gamma,* which are sometimes added to Secret or Top Secret materials raise the level of classification.

Classification Facts

- The classification system is put in place by presidential executive order. President Harry Truman issued the first order in 1940, and the most recent order was issued by President Barack Obama in 2009.
- The President, Vice President, heads of government agencies, and people appointed by these individuals may classify materials.
- The President receives the President's Daily Brief every morning—the classified intelligence report is delivered to the Oval Office in a locked briefcase.

- Currently, Executive order 13526, signed by President Barack Obama on December 29, 2009, provides specifics about classification.
- Typically, the top and bottom of documents are marked. Older documents may be marked at the top only, and very recent material may be marked paragraph by paragraph.
- Seventeen agencies form the Intelligence Community (IC) in the US.

Laws Protecting Classified Materials and Penalties for Illegal Acts

- The Espionage Act of 1917
- The Atomic Energy Act of 1954
- The Intelligence Identities Act of 1982.
- prison terms (1–10 years depending on situation)
- monetary fines ($1000–$10,000 depending on situation)

Organizations to Contact

The editors have compiled the following list of organizations concerned with the issues debated in this book. The descriptions are derived from materials provided by the organizations. All have publications or information available for interested readers. The list was compiled on the date of publication of the present volume; the information provided here may change. Be aware that many organizations take several weeks or longer to respond to inquiries, so allow as much time as possible for the receipt of requested materials.

American Civil Liberties Union (ACLU)
125 Broad Street, 18th Floor
New York, NY 10004
(212)-549-2500
website: www.aclu.org
The American Civil Liberties Union was started in 1920, and since its inception this organization has seen as its mission to be a guardian of liberty. The ACLU works in communities throughout the country, in courts, and in state legislatures to defend the rights of all citizens guaranteed by the Constitution and laws of the US. Its website is a resource and provides information and downloadable publications.

The American Enterprise Institute (AEI)
1789 Massachusetts Avenue, NW, Washington, DC 20036
(202)-862-5800
Fax: (202)-862-7177
website: www.aei.org/
The American Enterprise Institute is a nonprofit, public policy think tank. The AEI has been in Washington since 1943, and its staff and scholars shed light on issues dedicated to democracy, American strength and global leadership, and free enterprise. Its website features articles on a wide variety of topics and for college students, summer programs and internships are available.

Department of Homeland Security (DHS)

Secretary of Homeland Security
Washington, DC 20528
(202)-282-8000
website: www.dhs.gov

The Department of Homeland Security is a US governmental agency. The mission of DHS is to keep America safe and secure the nation against threats. The website maintained by the Department is a valuable resource. It provides information on a wide variety of topics including information on cybersecurity and issues related to classified intelligence.

Electronic Frontier Foundation (EFF)

815 Eddy Street
San Francisco, CA 94109
(415)-436-9333
Fax: (415)-436-9993
email: info@eff.org
website: www.eff.org

The Electronic Frontier Foundation is a nonprofit organization dedicated to protecting civil liberties in the digital world. The Foundation is comprised of a vast network of professionals working as reporters, attorneys, activists, and technologists, all working to defend free speech, advanced technologies, and to fight illegal surveillance programs. Besides research and reporting, the Foundation maintains guides, including tutorials on how to protect oneself from unwanted online surveillance.

Information Security Oversight Office (ISOO)

700 Pennsylvania Avenue, NW, Room 100
Washington, DC 20408-0001
(202)-357-5250
Fax: (202)-357-5907
email: isoo@nara.gov
website: www.archives.gov/isoo

The Information Security Oversight Office is a branch of the National Archives and Records Administration. The ISOO serves the President by managing classified and sensitive intelligence information. It also oversees the access to classified and declassified information when and where appropriate.

The National Archives and Records Administration (NARA)

8601 Adelphi Road
College Park, MD 20740-6001
(866)-272-6272
website: www.archives.gov
The National Archives and Records Administration is a depository for the records of the United States. Consequently, the agency and its webite is a rich resource about topics concerning classified information and intelligence.

National Security Agency (NSA)

9800 Savage Rd., Suite 6272
Ft. George G. Meade, MD 20755-6000
(301)-688-6311
website: www.nsa.gov
The National Security Agency/Central Security Service's mission is to protect US secrets, gain advantage against adversaries in cyberspace, and protect the privacy of American citizens. The agency, through its website, actively posts newly declassified intelligence information.

Office of the Director of National Intelligence (ODNI)

Office of the Inspector General of the Intelligence Community, Investigations Division, Reston 3
Washington, DC 20511
(855)-731-3260
Fax: (571)-204-8088
website: www.dni.gov
The Office of the Director of National Intelligence works to unify and integrate the intelligence community of the US. The Office directs projects concerning intelligence, counterterrorism, cyber threats and more.

For Further Reading

Books

Allen, Thomas B. *Declassified: 50 Top-Secret Documents That Changed History.* Washington, DC: National Geographic, 2008.

Details various espionage incidents and documents through history. Includes the Presidential Daily Brief that warned of an attack by Osama Bin Laden.

Bhattacharjee, Yudhijit. *The Spy Who Couldn't Spell: A Dyslexic Traitor, An Unbreakable Code, and the FBI's Hunt for America's Stolen Secrets*. New York, NY: New American Library, 2016.

Details the real-life case of how the FBI unraveled clues to hunt down and find an ingenious traitor by the name of Brian Regan.

Denson, Brian. *The Spy's Son: The True Story of the Highest Ranking CIA Officer Ever Convicted of Espionage and the Son He Trained to Spy for Russia.* New York, NY: Atlantic Monthly Press, 2015.

Follows the story of the CIA officer, Jim Nicholson and how he gave classified documents to Russian operatives. While in prison he trained his son to continue his illegal operations.

Edgar, Timothy H. *Beyond Snowden: Privacy, Mass Surveillance, and the Struggle to Reform the NSA*. Washington, DC: Brookings Institution Press, 2017.

Attempts to answer the question of what to do about mass surveillance programs in the US. Suggests ways to implement surveillance to keep US and its allies safe within our democracy.

Epstein, Edward J. *How America Lost Its Secrets: Edward Snowden, the Man and the Theft*. New York, NY: Alfred A. Knopf, 2017.

Rivetingly details the investigation into the story of Edward Snowden. Also illuminates how vulnerable the systems of national security in the US.

Friedman, Barry. *Unwarranted: Policing Without Permission*. New York, NY: Farrar, Straus and Giroux, 2017.

Written by an authority on constitutional law, this account melds topics of concern in today's society. Includes the issues of out-of-control policing, and secret governmental surveillance of Americans.

Gardner, Lloyd C. *The War on Leakers: National Security and American Democracy, from Eugene C. Debs to Edward Snowden.* New York, NY: The New Press, 2016.

Delves into the history of national security leakers. Debates the topics of national security, surveillance, and democracy.

Gup, Ted. *Nation of Secrets: The Threat to Democracy and the American Way of Life.* New York, NY: Doubleday, 2007.

Written by an investigative reporter to unveil the problem of American institutions keeping secrets from the American people that they serve. Details issues of security, privacy, and patriotism.

Jeffreys-Jones, Rhodri. *We Know All About You: The Story of Surveillance in Britain and America.* Oxford, UK: Oxford University Press, 2017.

Overview of surveillance in the US and Britain. Written by a historian and intelligence expert, it explores issues including intelligence agencies in the US and Britain, leaking of information, and surveillance.

Periodicals and Internet Sources

Bamford, James. "The Black-and-White Security Question," *Foreign Policy,* January/February 2015.

Byman, Daniel, and Wittes, Benjamin, "Reforming the NSA," Foreign Affairs, May/June, 2014. www.foreignaffairs.com/articles/united-states/2014-04-17/reforming-nsa.

Calabresi, Massimo, "Unmasking and Leaks: Trump's Russia Retort," Time, April 6, 2017. time.com/4728290/unmasking-leaks-trump-russia-retort/.

Calfas, Jennifer, "Stephen Colbert: President Trump's Leaker is Himself," Time, May 16, 2017. time.com/4780365/stephen-colbert-trump-russia/.

Chan, Melissa, "What to Know About Reality Leigh Winner, the Contractor Charged in Trump's First Leaking Case," Time, June 6, 2017. time.com/4807267/reality-leigh-winner-leak-nsa-contractor/.

Clapper, James R. "Why Black Lives Matter to US Intelligence," *Vital Speeches of the Day,* February, 2017.

Dumiak, Michael, "Pieces of a Paranoid Past," Scientific American, July 2007. www.scientificamerican.com/article/pieces-of-a-paranoid-past/.

Epstein, Edward Jay, "Why President Obama Can't Pardon Edward Snowden," Newsweek, January 5, 2017. www.newsweek.com/why-obama-wont-pardon-edward-snowden-nsa-538632.

Gajanan, Mahita, "U.S. Assigns Over 1,000 Spies to Protect the Rio Olympics," Time, August 5, 2016. time.com/4440416/us-spies-protect-olympics/.

Gladwell, Malcolm, "Daniel Ellsberg, Edward Snowden, and the Modern Whistle-Blower," The New Yorker, December 19 & 26, 2016. www.newyorker.com/magazine/2016/12/19/daniel-ellsberg-edward-snowden-and-the-modern-whistle-blower.

Graham, David A, "What Did Donald Trump Tell the Russians," The Atlantic, May 15, 2017. www.theatlantic.com/politics/archive/2017/05/trump-classified-information/526797/.

Kelly, Erin, "Congressional Investigators to Question Obama Administration Officials in Russia Probe," USA Today, October 12, 2017. www.usatoday.com/story/news/politics/2017/10/12/congressional-investigators-brormer-ag-loretta-lynch-and-former-un-ambassador-questioned-russia-prob/758645001/.

Kingsbury, Alex. "Government Secrecy: Does Greater Openness Threaten National Security," *CQ Researcher,* February 11, 2011.

Knickerbocker, Brad, "Bradley Manning: 'I'm Sorry My Actions Hurt the United States,'" The Christian Science Monitor, August 14, 2013. www.csmonitor.com/USA/Justice/2013/0814/Bradley-Manning-I-m-sorry-that-my-actions-hurt-the-United-States.

Levintova, Hannah, Vicens, A.J., Dejean, Ashley, "Hacker, Banker, Soldier, Spy: A Guide to the Key Players in the Trump-Russia Scandal," Mother Jones, June 1, 2017. www.motherjones.com/politics/2017/06/russia-trump-putin-scandal-key-players-dossiers/.

Miscik, Jami, "Intelligence and the Presidency," Foreign Affairs, May/June, 2017. www.foreignaffairs.com/articles/united-states/2017-04-17/intelligence-and-presidency.

O'Brien, David, "Half-Measures on Encryption Since Snowden," MIT Technology Review, January 25, 2016. www.technologyreview.com/s/545636/half-measures-on-encryption-since-snowden/.

Price, David H., "The New Surveillance Normal," Monthly Review, July/August 2014. monthlyreview.org/2014/07/01/the-new-surveillance-normal/.

Podesta, John, "The Hidden Threat: Combating Government Secrecy in the 21st Century," Center for American Progress, September 15, 2006. www.americanprogress.org/issues/general/news/2006/09/15/2182/the-hidden-threat-combating-government-secrecy-in-the-21st-century/.

Thorp, Frank V, "Barack Obama Signs 'USA Freedom Act' to Reform NSA Surveillance," NBC News, June 2, 2015. www.nbcnews.com/storyline/nsa-snooping/senate-vote-measure-reform-nsa-surveillance-n368341.

Web sites

Information Security Oversight Office

(www.archives.gov/isoo/faqs/identifying-handling-classified-records.html).
This website has questions and answers on classified information and how to handle documents containing this information.

Politico

(www.politico.com/gallery/2013/08/10-famous-infamous-whistleblowers-001083?slide=0).
This website displays portraits with short histories of ten whistle blowers that acted in business and government in the US.

USA Department of Defense

(www.usa.gov/federal-agencies/u-s-department-of-defense).
Search this website to find a rich source of information about the topic of classified intelligence.

Index

U

V

W

Y

Z

Picture Credits

Cover Anadolu Agency/Getty Images; p. 10 stable/Shutterstock.com; p. 13 Mario Tama/Getty Images; p. 18 Christian Delbert/Shutterstock.com; p. 23 Steve Hamann/Shutterstock.com; p. 31 New York Daily News Archive/Getty Images; p. 38 Mark Van Scyoc/Shutterstock.com; p. 45 jat306/iStock/Thinkstock; p. 49 Michael Blann/DigitalVision/Thinkstock; p. 51 Library of Congress Prints and Photographs Division; p. 59 Alexander Shcherbak/TASS/Getty Images; p. 66 Rena Schild/Shutterstock.com; p. 69 franz12/Shutterstock.com; p. 73 Alliance/Shutterstock.com; p. 76 Official White House Photo by Shealah Craighead/flickr.com/photos/whitehouse/36747062994; pp. 80, 93 Chip Somodevilla/Getty Images; p. 87 Paul Brady Photography/Shutterstock.com; p. 99 Sunshinepress/Getty Images.